By Beth Fe

See Mom Run

Side-Splitting Essays from the
World's Most Harried Moms

★ SeeMomRunBook.com ★

Copyright © 2009 Beth Feldman and Plain White Press LLC

All rights reserved. No portion of this book may be reproduced—mechanically, electronically, or by any other means, including photocopying—without written permission of the publisher.

Limit of Liability/Disclaimer of Warranty: The author and the publisher have made their best efforts in this book. The publisher and author make no claims to the accuracy and completeness of the information. The advice contained herein may not be appropriate for every individual. Neither the publisher nor the author shall be liable for any loss of profit or any other commercial damages.

ISBN 978-1-936005-02-4
Library of Congress Control Number: 2009934644

Design by Katie Schlientz

Plain White Press books are available at special discounts when purchased in bulk for premiums and sales promotions, as well as for fund-raising and educational use. Special editions or book excerpts can also be created to specifications. For details contact Publisher@PlainWhitePress.com.

plain white press™

dedication

This book is dedicated to the amazing mom bloggers, magazine writers, television producers, entrepreneurs, and grandmothers who shared lasting memories of motherhood that evolved into a rip-roaring anthology for parents. And thanks to my husband Darin, my children, Rebecca and Dylan, my parents, in-laws, and my grandparents, who have always encouraged me to follow my dreams. I love you all more than words can say.

table of contents

- x   **Introduction** by Beth Feldman
- 1   **Labor Daze** by Beth Feldman
- 7   **Baby Fat** by Danielle Dardashti
- 11   **There She Blows** by Jenna McCarthy
- 19   **Good Night? Yeah Right: "Nobody Sleeps Here"** by Jen Singer
- 23   **Bad Thai-ming** by Ciaran Blumenfeld
- 31   **Minivan Memoirs** by Dawn Meehan
- 35   **Do You Know the Muffin Top** by Tracy Beckerman, author of the syndicated humor column, *Lost in Suburbia*
- 41   **Fire Trucks Are Dangerous** by Issa M. Mas
- 47   **The Tooth Fairy, The Torah, and Me** by Nancy Friedman

table of contents

- 53 **Busy** by Abby Pecoriello

- 57 **The Traditional New York City Pedicure** by Jenny Baitch Isenman

- 61 **Fear of Flying** by Sara Fisher

- 67 **40th Birthday** by Eden Pontz

- 75 **The Isle of Needy, Scary, Screwed-Up, Misfit Toys** by Liz Gumbinner

- 79 **Eau de Colic** by Vanessa Druckman

- 83 **The Photo Shoot** by Melissa Chapman

- 87 **Pressing Rewind** by Andrea Forstadt

- 91 **The Harried Mom and Her Half-Trained Twins** by Cheryl Lage

- 95 **The Letter** by Sherry Shealy Martschink

- 99 **If it Looks Like A Duck** by Beth Feldman

- 103 **Night of Horror, i.e. The Night the Wireless Went Out** by Beth Blecherman

- 107 **The Secret** by Meredith Jacobs

- 113 **Busted** by April Welch, CPO

119 **A Trip to Remember** by Jeanne Muchnick

125 **Empty Nesters** by Janie Lam Meyers

129 **Tests** by Lenore Stoller

131 **Run Nana Run** by Sue Levine Kupcinet

135 **The Sanitation Mom** by Beth Feldman

139 **Type B Mom** by Liz Gumbinner

143 **To Clean or Not to Clean?** by Jenny Baitch Isenman

147 **Airing my Dirty Laundry** by Lenore Stoller

151 **The Final Addition** by Beth Feldman

157 **Author Bios**

introduction

I have always been a storyteller at heart. And when I became a mom, my life became an open book. For the past several years, I have chronicled my most memorable, harried, and oftentimes embarrassing moments on RoleMommy.com, an online community and events company dedicated to inspiring parents to pursue their passions while raising a family.

During that time, the blogosphere has led me to some of the most talented humor writers I have ever met. From those who craft cleverly written Twitter one-liners, to essayists who wax nostalgic about the pitfalls of parenting, I knew the ideal way to capture every aspect of motherhood would be to tap into some of the best storytellers I know.

As I reached out one by one to the writers whose work I admired from afar to be a part of *See Mom Run*, I was blown away by the response. Every single one of my favorite "Role Mommies" agreed to share their memorable stories.

Far more exciting, when I introduced them virtually, the conversation nearly had me falling out of my chair. As they bantered back and forth over who had dibs on the best potty or puke story, what I came to learn was that all of us shared a common bond. At the heart of it, we are moms who have found a way to make light of some of the most stressful moments of our lives.

From there, I began to craft a collection of stories that every mom could relate to, whether you've just given birth or have said good-bye to your children as they've finally left the nest. With the help of the nation's most talented humor bloggers, television producers, magazine writers, an organization expert, a retired senator, two grandmothers, and many more, *See Mom Run* captures all those harried moments of our lives with candor, wit, and a little wisdom thrown in for good measure.

So dear reader, it's time for you to dive in. If you have a personal parenting parable you'd like to share or if you'd like to attend a *See Mom Run* event in your area, then visit us at RoleMommy.com and find out how you can be a part of the action.

Key

Twitter   Facebook   Text Message   Email

labor daze

By Beth Feldman ★ Role Mommy

Really, do you have to weigh a woman when she's about to give birth? Why the painful reminder that I am now the size of a small planet?

Every mom has one. Whether it's a scheduled C-section, water that breaks on a subway platform, contractions in a snowstorm. Heck, there are even tales of women who didn't make it to the hospital in time and delivered in a taxicab. Or, the stories of those brave souls who managed to birth a ten-pound baby in a bathtub. And let's not forget the fertile women who have popped out twins, triplets, quadruplets, or that infamous octomom.

And then there's me. As birthing stories go, I've managed to experience both sides of the spectrum. While both were technically "natural" deliveries (with an epidural to take the edge off), the first time, I made it all the way to my due date and then found myself playing the waiting game ... for 72 hours.

My friend Holli told me I would know the exact moment when I was going into labor. Here's how she described it: "You're going to feel a lot of bruising down below your groin. OK, now picture taking a jack hammer and slamming down hard on that bruise. Over, and over, and over again!" Truth be told, Holli was absolutely right.

Luckily, my parents were at my house the morning my labor had begun so when my husband went to work, they hovered over me as I tried to take my mind off the pain and not call the doctor until my contractions were less than seven minutes apart. Of course, the moment I reached that benchmark, I started dialing the phone.

"Dr. G., I think it's time for me to go to the hospital. I've been having contractions all day and now they are taking place every five minutes." Well actually, maybe it was every ten or eleven minutes, but what's a little fudging of the facts between a doctor and a patient? I'll tell you what. When he finally gave me the green light to head to the hospital, we hopped in our SUV, raced into Manhattan, were whisked into the maternity ward and within ten minutes, were sent packing.

You see, I had only dilated 1 centimeter. And I needed to get to 10 friggin' centimeters!!! How could that be? I was in agony. But my body wouldn't budge. And my doctor was resting comfortably at home, recuperating from back surgery the week prior. While he didn't meet me at the hospital, Dr. G. did summon enough energy to talk me down off the ceiling and send me back to my Subaru.

And so we went home. And the contractions worsened. At one point, I was so uncomfortable, I found myself lying in a fetal position with my head in the cat bed. I couldn't take it anymore. So we drove back to Manhattan. And we arrived at the maternity ward. And they examined me. And they sent me back home.

This happened four times over the course of three days. And by the third time, there was no way I was going back over the Tri Boro bridge, bumping over pot holes and fighting traffic to spend another sleepless night sharing a sherpa pillow with my two Maine Coons. Instead, my best friend Beth invited us over to her Upper East Side apartment where she threw my family a "Labor Party." As everyone spent the day munching on nachos and crudité, I sat in a comfy, oversized shabby chic chair, sucking on ice chips and digging my fingers into the upholstery. Sadly, after being sent home a fourth time from the hospital (I had advanced to 1.5 centimeters), we arrived back at Beth's apartment at midnight where I labored from 1 until 5 a.m. As I moaned and groaned in a semi-conscious state of delirium, I honed in on a Picasso reproduction on the wall, and proceeded to wail and kick my husband in the groin when I couldn't bear the pain any longer. In a matter of 24 hours, I pretty much turned Beth off to childbirth for at least a decade.

As daylight finally approached, we were on a mission to get admitted. And this time, since I had finally reached 4 centimeters, the intern on duty took pity upon me and signed me into the maternity ward. In fact, the nurses felt so bad they had turned me away so many times that they put me in the swankiest birthing suite at New York Hospital complete with a view of the Hudson River and over 1000 square feet that I didn't really need unless I was inviting all my relatives inside to catch the big moment. And finally, after what must have been my 200th contraction, the anesthesiologist arrived and within seconds, I was in heaven. We spent several more hours waiting and watching my contractions erupt on screen and then by 4 p.m., I was finally ready to push and the doctor was nowhere to be found. Ten minutes later, Dr. G. re-emerged just as my daughter, made her grand entrance into the world and life as we knew it was never going to be the same.

THE FLIP SIDE: Fast forward three years and I've got three weeks left until my due date. I've got a mountain of work piling up at the office, it's the end of the fall television season and I'm planning press schedules for four major prime time shows. Three days earlier, I spent at least ten hours on my feet with a cranky cast of a sitcom who, by the end of the shoot, wanted to punch each other out. And me, I feel like a baby hippo because this time around, I've gained 42 pounds and I'm only 5'1".

So it's Monday morning and I'm ready to start my day where I was going to meet an elderly actor on a train platform on the Lower East Side for a video shoot with *Extra*, when "BAM!" I feel that bruising/jack hammer sensation that Holli had warned me about a few years earlier. Uh-oh. This can't be good.

I dismiss the searing pain and think to myself, "Well, if this is anything like the last go round, it's going to take at least three days before this kid arrives, so I've got plenty of time." Wishful thinking.

Since my husband was already at work (do you see a pattern here?), I asked Holli if she'd take me to the doctor's office and she was at my house within seconds. After the examination, they told me I had already reached four centimeters, and, if I preferred, I could labor at home for a few more hours or head straight to the hospital. While I was further along, I thought there was no way this baby was going to arrive that fast. So we went to the diner—where I ate French onion soup and white knuckled the table when the contractions hit. When a woman asked Holli if I was in labor, my devoted friend shook her head yes and shrugged her shoulders. Meanwhile, since I was in complete denial, I called my parents, who were about an hour and a half away and told them to take their time, there was no way I was going to be giving birth that day. Thankfully, they didn't listen.

After the diner, Holli decided to do a bagel run. Unbeknownst to me, she was totally stalling because she didn't want to drop me off at home until my parents arrived. And after she had ordered two dozen bagels, a half a pound of lox, a container of cream cheese, and I had been walloped by two more contractions, Holli drove back to my house and my mom was there to welcome me with open arms.

Of course, I still had several loose ends I had to wrap up. And so, every two minutes I would fire off an e-mail to my assistant before I would double over in excruciating pain. As I sent messages with my left hand while gripping the wall with my right, I managed to get most of the items crossed off of my to-do list. Top priority: find famous celebrity senior citizen on subway platform and make sure someone escorts him to video shoot. Once I knew he was in good hands, and my husband came home from work, I was ready to hit the hospital.

Once we arrived, the emergency room attendant saw my deranged look and directed us to the maternity ward where they took my blood and weighed me. Really. Do you have to weigh a woman when she's about to give birth? Why the painful reminder that I am now the size of a small planet and my husband, whom I hadn't shared this piece of embarrassing news with, gets to see the final tally (as he fondly recalls—"Wow, a buck 62... that's pretty large").

As the contractions grew more intense, I almost missed the window where I could receive an epidural and just as I thought I was going to experience natural childbirth against my will, the doctor arrived with that two-foot long needle.

Within minutes, my water broke and I was ready to birth me a baby boy.

And then, with only two pushes, I heard cheers from the crowd as my son flew out of me as if he were a football and I had scored a winning touchdown by passing him safely to my OB GYN. Within minutes, they cleaned him up, wrapped him in a blanket and placed him on my chest. And at that very moment, I instantly fell in love with a new little man.

baby fat

by Danielle Dardashti

Being asked, "When are you due?" before saying you're pregnant: Bad. Being asked, "When are you due?" five months after you have the baby: Worse.

It happened to me the other day at the supermarket.

As I stood in the checkout line, the sweet Jamaican clerk smiled at me a heck of a lot and complimented my necklace. Then, as I was signing my credit card slip, it happened.

She asked, "When's the baby coming?" And for a split second I thought she was asking me when I was going to bring the baby by the store. But how would she have known I'd recently had a baby? Then I realized what she meant.

I looked up at her, and with great pause said, "I'm not pregnant. I gave birth five months ago." And patting my belly, I said apologetically, "I'm working on it."

The guy behind me in line shook his head either out of sympathy, or just because he didn't have anything to say. I don't know.

I headed out of the supermarket feeling really fat. As I caught a glimpse of my post-baby-number-two reflection in the store window, I sucked in my stomach and decided it was time to take the bull by the horns and try to start looking like my old self again.

But which "old self"?

My 24-year-old pre-marriage-skinny self?

My 29-year-old pre-babies-but-not-quite-so-skinny-anymore self?

My 31-year-old post-baby-number-one/pre-baby-number-two, not-quite-fat-but-slightly-zaftig self?

Who am I?

As I pondered the existential on my way out of the Toco Hills Kroger in Atlanta, I was pretty ticked off about the sweet checkout lady's lack of tact. And I wished I hadn't been so nice and apologetic about it all. But what could I have said?

My friend Marla Shavin says she had a similar experience a few months after her second child, Adam, was born.

She was working as a producer at WXIA-TV, Channel 11. The culprit was a guest on *Noonday*—a female magazine editor who Marla describes as "all about women empowering themselves."

Marla says, "She popped the question on me. And I'll never forget her exact words. She said, 'Are you with child?'"

Marla, who is now the mother of three beautiful children, says that if she had been truly empowered by this woman, she would have responded: "Are you with brain?!" She says, "Who asks that question without 101% certainty?! I want to see the doctor's chart or the EPT results before I say anything!"

Our pediatrician, Michal Loventhal, says she and her husband Gary (also a pediatrician) have a pact that they never ask anyone that question, no matter how obviously pregnant the woman may look. And they both see lots of women every day who are in that baby-making stage of their lives.

Michal says, "Even if she's a stick with a basketball stomach, unless the woman brings it up herself, I don't say anything about it."

But she recently gave birth to her second child Talia. And, sure enough, it happened to Michal, too.

A couple months after Talia was born, Michal was at Gymboree with her two-year-old daughter, Ellie. She was talking to a woman who was there with her baby.

Michal asked the woman how old her baby was. The woman answered, and then asked, "When's your baby due?" Michal responded, "Months ago!" and explained that her baby was already almost two months old.

The woman apologized profusely, but the damage had already been done.

Another woman there reassured Michal that she looked great, and said, "That woman has the social skills of a doorknob!"

Though Michal shrugged it off, she agrees that it does hurt when that happens. "You just want to shrink back to your normal self," she says, "but it doesn't usually happen that way."

Is it merely coincidence that it happened to all of us after our second baby?

Perhaps what was, after our first baby, a cute little "pooch," is better described as "blubber" after giving birth to our second.

But maybe it's something else, too.

The second time around, we're less put-together. In our

rush to take care of everyone else, we tend to neglect ourselves, even more than we did the first time.

We're more likely to run out of the house without having looked in the mirror once that day; more likely to just throw on an old maternity shirt when the shirt we were planning to wear gets covered with the baby's spit-up or the toddler's peanut butter and jelly.

Come to think of it, I was wearing a very loose outfit that day at the supermarket. One that I bought right after the baby was born. Probably too big for me now, five months later.

Michal thinks she may have been wearing a maternity shirt that day at Gymboree.

And Marla says she doesn't remember exactly what she was wearing the day that lady popped the question. "It was winter," she says. "Maybe something velour. Definitely something with elastic waist, you know, that post-partum look?"

She has three kids now, so it's a miracle she still remembers anything.

there she blows

by Jenna McCarthy

"Jenna has locked her cat in the bathroom with a humidifier and wonders if this is normal."

"Who's ready to go have some fun?" I chirped, buckling my darlings into their car seats. It was a perfect summer day, balmy and clear, and we were headed to the water park. Never mind that I would rather drink my own bath water than appear in public in a bathing suit, or that I had gotten my period that morning and felt like a pregnant whale. I'm a mom and I promised and the girls had been talking about nothing else for weeks. I'd stashed a half a box of super-plus tampons in my bag, swallowed a handful of Motrin and was feeling only moderately Shamu-like in my trusty tankini. If I sucked in my gut with all my might, only a small roll of flesh actually wiggled through the window between top and bottom. Screw it, I told myself, tying on the sarong that made this outfit bearable. It's not like anyone would be looking at me anyway.

About midway into the 45-minute drive, five-year-old Sophie announced that her tummy hurt.

"It's OK sweetie," I told her. "I get kind of queasy in the car sometimes, too. Roll down your window and get some fresh air. That will make you feel better."

Sophie, who has an unnatural (for her tender age) obsession with her hair and its perfection, actually obliged. Had I been paying closer attention, I might have taken this as a sign of the situation's gravity.

"I think I'm going to puke," she announced, pulling her disheveled head back in the window.

Since neither of my kids had ever gotten sick in the car before, and since I was busily jamming to Gwen Stefani (I know; I'm a horrible mother. We should have been listening to the Wiggles but don't worry, there are consequences coming), I admit I didn't take this all that seriously.

"I really am going to puke," Sophie added, starting to sound a little frantic.

I turned around in my seat and saw her holding both hands in front of her mouth, cheeks puffed up, looking very much like she was about to blow.

And then she did.

All over the car.

"Gross, mom, it stinks!" three-year-old Sasha wailed from the seat next to her. I mean clearly, Sophie had violently regurgitated her breakfast as part of an ongoing plot to annoy her sister.

Sasha was right. It really, really stank.

I found it hard to believe that Sophie's tiny stomach could hold the volume of vomit that was now splattered across the back seat like blood in a Scorsese movie. Chunks clung to the backs of both front seats and sloshed across the floor boards. Barf oozed over and around and into every crevice of her car seat and the bench beneath her and slid lava-like down the door. It appeared that every partially-digested bite of food she'd put into her mouth in the past month was now Jackson Pollock'd about the car's interior.

I sped up to 85 miles an hour (like you wouldn't have done the same thing), desperate to find a spot on the endless stretch of highway to pull over. While Sasha moaned and whined and kicked in an effort to make sure everyone in the car knew that there were noxious fumes assaulting her delicate nostrils, Sophie to her enormous credit sat quietly cupping the dripping remains of her scrambled eggs. I'm one of those people who can easily puke at the mere sight of puke, a decided disadvantage in times like this, so I kept my eyes on the road and tried to think of something more pleasant. Sadly, the aroma in the car kept bringing me back to the rotting pelican carcass we had happened upon last week at the beach.

Breathe through your mouth, I told myself, trying not to imagine airborne puke-particles floating in the car.

Finally, we came to a turn-out and I pulled over. As a parade of trucks roared past us, showering us with dusty, pebbly grit, I gently lifted (OK, frantically ripped) the girls from their car seats and installed them in a sandy patch of gravel as far from the road as possible. Then I began searching for something—anything—to clean up the mess with. You'll be happy to know that if I ever found myself in a French-fry emergency, I'd have enough ketchup packets in my glove box to accompany a dozen or more king-size orders. Should the lenses spontaneously pop out of my sunglasses, I could have my choice of any of the seven only slightly-scratched replacement pairs on hand. But a freaking napkin? An old diaper? A dehydrated, shoe-print stained, Cheeto-crusted wet wipe? None of the above. Damning myself for opting to indulge in the water park's rental-towel program rather than bringing some from home, I thought about unwrapping a few tampons and tossing them on the floor to absorb some of the liquid, but I was pretty sure I was going to need every last one in my stash. The only scrap of paper or fabric in the entire vehicle was the sarong around my lower half. Removing it would mean I'd have to walk practically bare-assed into the godforsaken water park, but what choice did I have? I reluctantly removed it, turned it inside out and used it to wipe Sophie down, cursing myself again, this time for not being one of those clever, forward-thinking moms who always has a roll of Bounty and a bottle of Febreeze on hand for emergencies. I tore the sopping cover from her car seat and wadded it into a disgusting ball, marching around to the back of the car to toss it in the trunk.

"I'm sorry, mom," mumbled a forlorn-looking Sophie. I stopped cleaning and knelt in the dirt before her, cupping her flushed face in my sticky hands, my ass-crack boldly displayed for the entire highway-driving world to enjoy.

"Honey, you never have to be sorry for being sick," I scolded gently, overwhelmed with guilt that I didn't think to say this sooner. "I'm the one who's sorry for not listening to you!"

"No, mom," she said, shaking her head. "I was going to say I'm sorry that you just stepped in dog poo."

Effing great.

Picture, if you will, this: A filthy homeless-looking woman, driving along in her bathing suit, wearing only one shoe. A naked five year old, swaddled about the bottom in a damp, smelly scrap of cotton-spandex, strapped into the hard plastic base of a car seat. A pissed-off three year old, clamping her nostrils shut with one hand. This is how we drove for the next 15 miles, all of the windows down, until we saw the sign heralding salvation: Target! Exit now! (For those of you who may not believe in God, I am here to tell you He exists. There really wasn't a Target there the last time I drove this stretch. I swear it.)

At this point, I had a choice to make: I could march my half-naked self into the mother of all megastores and walk out with fresh, puke-free clothes and poo-less shoes, plus enough chlorofluorocarbons to kill an SUV full of odious germs. Or I could take the same scantily-clad self straight to the water park and hand-wash the soiled items in a public sink that could possibly leave them more contaminated after a scrubbing, while the stinky vomit remains boiled and festered and multiplied all day in the car under the scorching summer sun.

Bull's-eye.

I once fell off a stage at a concert, landing squarely (and with a thunderous echo) at the feet of a row of people who moments before had probably been peering up my skirt, now that I think about it. Another time, while working at a job I very much liked at a high-profile national magazine, I wrote a scathingly nasty e-mail about my boss and accidently sent it to my boss. Rest assured that neither of these utterly mortifying episodes or the dozens more that instantly leap to mind could touch the humiliation I felt as I slunk (make that stunk) into Tar-zhay.

I had managed to scrape the majority of the crap off of my shoe, but the distinctive scent lingered. I had an oversized, equally foul-smelling and inexplicably swaddled child on my hip and another smaller one clinging desperately to the side of my bathing suit, pulling it ever lower despite my repeated hissing to *get her effing hands off of it.* I tried to walk confidently, but all I could think was Dear God Almighty, my jiggly, dimply ass is on public, fluorescently-lit display. If you have ever felt this particular sort of body anxiety, say at a pool or the beach, I assure you that it is only magnified eight or nine billion times when you are thusly clad in a place where everyone else's below-the-belt region is completely covered.

Wiggle, swish, jiggle.

Someone, please shoot me.

I tried to avoid the rubber-necked stares (have you *been* to Target on a Saturday?) as I marched to the ladies department and grabbed the first slip-on skirt my fingers could find. Leaving the tags prominently displayed ("I wasn't going to steal it officer! You see, we had a little accident on the way here . . .") we slugged through the store, collecting the rest of the day's necessities (plus a really nice sisal rug I needed for the patio and some darling thank-you notes that practically leapt into the cart.) A buck-fifty later, we were back in the Stink Mobile (which now smelled like someone had merely regurgitated an ocean of Summer Mist in it—a vast improvement).

"I'm hungry," Sophie announced, before I even put the car into reverse.

"My tummy hurts," Sasha chimed in.

For the record, in case you were wondering, Target does not have a bar. I checked.

"Girls, we are exactly nine minutes from the water park and almost an hour from home," I told them, trying to muster up my last reluctant ounce of calm. "Which is it going to be?"

We finally made it to the water park and actually had a fantastic day. The water was frigid, the food was crappy and ridiculously overpriced, but no one got sunburned or drowned, no one (that I saw) pointed or laughed at my ass, and no one (in my care) forcibly ejected the contents of her stomach out of her mouth. There wasn't a single nanosecond of whining from either of my children, and they both had Bozo-like grins plastered to their faces for six solid hours.

As we were waiting our turn to shuffle through the exit turnstile, Sophie spontaneously grabbed my hand.

"Thanks for the best day ever, mom," she said, squeezing my fingers three times, our secret code for "I love you." I looked down at the beaming, bleary-eyed, sun-kissed faces of my two dazzling daughters, then at my bejeweled $13 flip-flop score from the morning's unplanned Target run.

"It was a pretty great day, wasn't it?" I said, squeezing back four times ("I love you, too.").

We rode all the way home with the windows down. The girls slept the entire time; Gwen cursed softly in the background. By the time we pulled into the driveway, my eyes had almost stopped watering from the wind-whipped chemical cocktail circulating inside the car.

"New shoes?" their dad asked, first thing, upon our return. Not "How was it?" or "Did you have fun?" or "Why do the girls have Kramer hair?" The man is a hound, I tell you. His nose can pick up new product smell from four miles away.

"Yup," I replied. "They cost a hundred and fifty bucks and they were worth every penny."

He artfully lifted an eyebrow, studying the I-dare-you-to-ask look on my face.

"They're cute," he said simply.

"I think so, too," I agreed.

good night?
yeah right: "nobody sleeps here"

By Jen Singer ★ Momma Said

> Blogging is like breastfeeding: The more you do it, the more you can produce.

I couldn't tell her the truth. I couldn't tell her "Nobody sleeps here." So, when my neighbor, Janet, then pregnant with her first, asked if she could sleep over while her husband was away on business, I simply said, "Yes," when, really, I wanted to ask, "OK, but can I stay at your house?"

It was kind of cute how vulnerable Janet was that night. She didn't want to be home alone, figuring that staying overnight in my full house would give her that warm, safe feeling she hadn't had since she stopped being able to break into a sprint, not long after her first ultrasound.

That night, Janet and I stayed up and chatted for a bit, and, apparently, so did my children. I could hear them on their baby monitors, and I could feel it already: This was gonna be a long night.

Janet got ready for bed and then waddled into the guest room and shut the door. My husband and I went to our room, but not for long. Our not-quite-three-year-old son, Nicholas, called me. "Moooooomyyyyyy!" I skidded down the hall and tried to shush him, but he knew: House guests mean no sleep for the big people.

I scooped him up and brought him into my bed where I figured the three of us would fall asleep. That's when my toddler, Christopher, started to cry. I raced down the hall, picked him up before he could work himself into a full-out wail, and brought him back to my bed where I figured the four of us would fall asleep. I suppose it was kind of cute how vulnerable I was.

It wasn't long before Nicholas elbowed me and Christopher kicked him and soon, everyone pushed Daddy off the bed. It was like Friday Night Smackdown in footy pajamas. It was a work night, so my husband ditched us to get some sleep in Nicholas' room, while I started to wonder where Janet kept her house keys.

For the next few hours, I would beg, plead, and bribe my kids to go to sleep. I filled and refilled bottles. (And so, I changed and re-changed diapers.) I'd get one to almost nod off, and then the other one would wake him up. I felt like Lucille Ball trying to keep the chocolates on the conveyer belt. It just wouldn't stop.

Finally, my baby fell asleep. I thought his big brother had dozed off, too, until I heard a faint, "Where's my crayon?" Nicholas had been holding a green crayon all night and, apparently, he couldn't go to sleep without it.

"I'll get you one in the morning," I mumbled.

"Where's my crayon?" he asked more loudly. My toddler twitched, but fell back asleep.

"Shhhh. I'll get you an entire new box in the morning," I promised. "Sixty-four crayons with a sharpener."

"I want my crayon!" he raised his voice. His brother grimaced, but kept sleeping.

"I will drive you to the Crayola Factory tomorrow and get you whatever you want. Just please, PLEASE, go to sleep!" I clenched my teeth, calculating how long it would take me to drive to Pennsylvania to buy crayons.

"I WANT MY CRAYON!" he shouted, and with that, his brother awoke.

"WAAAAAAAAA!"

My toddler cried. His brother cried. I cried. It was now 3 o'clock in the morning, and I hadn't slept at all, and yet, I wasn't at a keg party or vacationing in a different time zone.

I picked them both up and carried them downstairs where I refilled their bottles yet again. We wrapped ourselves in blankets and curled up on the couch. I figured that the three of us would just fall asleep there. And then, that's when I heard it: BEEP. BEEP. BEEP. BEEP.

Our phone had broken earlier that day (or really, the day before), and though it was unplugged, it beeped incessantly, like a scene from a *Twilight Zone* episode where the appliances try to take over the Earth, or a garbage truck yard at 5 a.m.

EEP. BEEP. BEEP. BEE... I jumped up off the couch, threw open the kitchen window and hurled the phone into the backyard. Then I closed the window, got back on the couch, wrapped everyone up in blankets and tried to go to sleep.

BEEP. BEEP. BEEP. The phone was beeping in the backyard in the snow and my kids were still wide awake. So, I did what any desperate mother would do: I bundled my boys in their snowsuits, warmed up the car and took them for a ride around the neighborhood at 4 a.m.

Nobody was out. Not a car. Not a deer. Not a squirrel. Not another mother trying to get her kids to go to sleep. My car thermometer read 11 degrees. I thanked God that my mother-in-law didn't live in my town.

Finally, my baby fell asleep. I drove home, pulled him out of his car seat (but not his snowsuit) and placed him in my bed. Then I put Nicholas, drowsy but awake, in the bed next to him, and climbed under the covers. I started to doze off when...

"WHERE'S MY CRAYON?!"

"WAAAAAAAAAAAAAAAAAAAAAA!"

I marched down the hall, poked at my husband like a cop trying to move a drunk from the bank's front door, and barked, "It's 5 o'clock in the morning! I have been awake all night! It's your turn, buster."

Without a word, he shuffled down the hall, climbed into our bed and all three of them fell right asleep. I, on the other hand, was wide awake.

The next morning (a.k.a. 90 minutes later), my husband was brushing his teeth when he glanced out the window and spotted our phone in the snow. He thought, "What the..." and then, "Ooooooh." He knew exactly how that phone had wound up in the backyard. He shrugged and went back to brushing his teeth.

When Janet came downstairs, I apologized for all the commotion the night before. She swore she heard nothing, but I noticed that the next time her husband went away on business, she stayed home alone. If only she had invited me to stay overnight.

bad thai-ming

By Ciaran Blumenfeld

False Alarm! My dd does not have lice. She does have a little dandruff. And a lot of glitter.

As a mom of four I embrace chaos, mess, and the certain knowledge that no matter what I do, I'm probably screwing someone up for life. But once upon a time, I had all the answers. I was blissfully, obnoxiously confident. I knew it all. I was the mother of one child.

My first daughter M. was what I now recognize as extremely easy. She was one of those rare mythical babies that goes to sleep the instant they are laid down, takes two naps a day, rarely throws a tantrum and is not a picky eater. Naturally I credited all of this to my superior parenting skills and possibly even a supernatural talent for raising kids. Was it possible to be a mommy savant? I faux-kvetched with my pals about the hardships of motherhood. But honestly? The hardest it got was when she cut a tooth and her usual ten hours of sleep were reduced to eight.

Feel free to hate me because I was one of those moms who scrapbooked, and never forgot a sweater in case it got chilly. My darling, perfect daughter's hair bows and shoes always matched her outfits. It wouldn't last of course, but I had a good run. Things started to fall apart when I got pregnant with my second. Karma was coming for me and my perfectly packed designer diaper bag.

M. was two and a half when I got pregnant. I read a stack of parenting books on adjusting to siblings and quickly became an "expert" on the topic. I decided the key to her psychological well-being would be to establish a routine and friends of her own that would stay the same after the baby arrived. I enrolled her in preschool. However, in order to be in the "big kid" class come fall, M. had to be fully potty-trained.

Piece of cake, I thought. I had also read every potty-training book. I invested in sparkly sticker charts, and bought a potty that played a cheerful song when you "flushed." Of course, I had a drawer full of pretty little incentive panties festooned with her favorite princesses.

I'd heard talk at the playground about how trying potty-training could be. Other moms traded tales about how difficult it was to get their kids potty-trained. But those were the same moms who packed yucky preservative-laden snacks for their kids and forgot the Purell, weren't they? Their kids called other kids "Poo-Poo-Head" and picked their noses. No wonder those parents were having a tough time. Maybe they were inconsistent? Or just plain lazy? Not that I was judgmental or anything. I just did not anticipate these types of problems.

As with most things concerning M., we enjoyed nearly immediate success. M. was actually happy to use the potty, wear the princess panties and quickly graduated to the big potty. Until the day we took her to Disneyland.

In my defense, none of the potty-training books I had read had a chapter about self-flushing public toilets, and the lasting damage they can do to a child's fragile psyche. One ill-timed splashy whoosh in the Magic Kingdom loo and my daughter decided she was never pooping on the pot again.

Days went by and my daughter refused to poop. One night she wept and pled for a diaper, and I gave in. My husband was leaving town on a work trip and I really wasn't up to an extended battle. Thus a diaper was dispatched; my daughter disappeared under the dining room table to do her business and then came back sheepishly, asking to be changed. She'd gone, but only a little. A mere pebble. We did not speak of this to anyone. We two were complicit in our grim silence. It was our dirty little secret.

Over the course of the next week, I offered the diaper again, several times. I figured we'd get back on track with the big potty when my husband was home to help out. My princess retreated under the dining room table with her diaper each evening. And each evening she produced little more than a pea. I was actually grateful that she didn't go very much. Less mess for me.

Towards the end of my solo-parenting week, I was more tired than usual. I missed my husband. If he'd been home I would have sent him out for Thai food. On a whim I called a childless friend of mine. We hadn't spoken in ages and she was happy to meet me for dinner.

My friend was not too fond of, or comfortable with, small

children. But I reassured her that M. was exceptionally well-behaved at restaurants.

"People take their kids to nice restaurants in Europe all the time, just a matter of parental expectation," I explained.

We freshened up and dressed for our dinner. Recklessly confident, my daughter and I both wore white eyelet.

My friend was waiting, cocktail in hand, when we arrived at the Thai place. The swanky restaurant was dimly lit and packed with couples. I wondered why we didn't go out more often with M. Had we just gotten complacent? Fallen prey to the message that having kids meant only going out to "family friendly" dining places? How had this happened to me? I looked forward to introducing M. to Pad Thai. Sans peanut and shrimp, of course, "It's best to wait until they're at least three," I explained to my friend.

"Ummm . . . right," she nodded, "I heard a lot of kids are allergic to peanuts and it causes autism or something?"

Quickly she changed the subject. She wanted to tell me about her latest conquest, a businessman she'd met in the airport and bedded in a nearby hotel. I covered M.'s ears and let her stand on the bench, normally verboten, but the story was getting juicy.

M. bounced a little and I told her to settle down. She whined she was thirsty and made for the large stemmed glass of water on the table in front of her. Quickly I flagged the waiter, to fetch us a to-go cup and straw. He gave me a concerned look as M. flung a contraband ice cube into the booth behind ours. I was mortified; it was so totally out of character! But of course I had a plan. It was time for her to sit and color with the crayons I had so cleverly packed.

Moments later M. was on her feet again. She was doing a little dance on the bench and pulling my hair. My friend's story was getting better. It involved an impromptu flight to Paris and jewels.

"Shhh, shhhhhh...." I urged M. to stop bouncing. "Sit on your bottom honey." I gave her my "mommy means business" look.

M. dropped back down onto her knees, and picked up a crayon, half-heartedly. My friend continued.

" So... I wasn't exactly surprised when he told me about his wife," she said. "But their marriage was over a while ago. Total bitch."

My brain made that screechy record stopping sound that you hear on TV when the heroine realizes something is amiss.

"Wait. What?! Wife?! Did you just say wife? Please tell me there were no kids..."

M.'s crayon rolled off the table and under the booth. She dove to retrieve it. My friend sipped her drink and sighed... "Well that's just the thing...," she began, "I think that's why he's stayed in the marriage so long. Damn rugrats..."

My pal droned on about her dangerous liaison with the married French dad. I only thought of my own husband, also traveling on business. I began to wish I'd ordered in.

Under the table M. whimpered and pulled at my skirt.

"I'll get you another crayon honey. Just don't touch anything under there! Let me get a wipey."

I scooped M. onto my lap. She was warm, and wriggly, refusing to stay still for some reason. I stroked her hair, trying to calm her as I scrambled in my bag for a couple of wipes.

"You're sure you don't need to go potty honey?" my friend asked M., over enunciating as if she were speaking to a deaf foreigner.

"She tinkled at home before we came," I answered. I didn't bother to correct M. when she stuck out her tongue at my friend.

Finally, the waiter arrived with our food. And at the precise moment he set it down, M. bolted to her feet. There was a strange noise. A squeaky, squelchy, rumble. Was it my stomach rumbling? Was it the sound of her rubber-soled sandals on the vinyl booth bench? The plate of noodles steamed in front of me. It smelled wrong somehow. And then I felt the warmth. The wet.

My friend saw my face and thought something was wrong with the dish.

"What is it? Did they put on peanuts? Shrimp? We can send it back . . ." and then, " PU! Jesus. Is that your dish? What smells so funny? Is that fish paste?"

I can only describe the scene on my side of the booth as a shit storm. I looked down at the liquid feces puddling on the bench. A waterfall of crap cascaded over the vinyl seat, pooling on the floor. My lap, the bottom of my bag, the back of M.'s dress and the whole front of mine were soaked. M. cowered against me, shaking. I was still clutching the two wipes that I'd used to protect her from the germs under the table. They too were soaked in shit. It was unfathomable how so much shit could come out of a child that small. Yet it continued to flow, like hot stinking lava.

"Umm, hello? Are you OK?" My friend asked.

Diners turned their heads and sniffed the air as they tried to place the foul odor. It was bad. Third-world-public-restroom bad.

"I think my daughter just exploded," I whispered.

My friend rolled her eyes. "Ew. That's so gross, this is why I am glad I don't have kids," she said. "You want my napkin?"

"No, I mean really! She EXPLODED!" I hissed. My friend set her drink down, half stood and peered across the booth. Her eyes bugged and she struggled not to vomit. I could see the fight or flight response kicking in. She looked around nervously for the exit. "I really gotta get out of here. I don't think . . . I can't . . . do this . . ." she said.

"Hold up a minute, home-wrecker, you're not going anywhere." I said, "Don't you dare abandon me here. I need you to reach in my bag and get the $100 bill out of my wallet."

Cagily she reached into my bag, and pulled out the wallet with two manicured fingers. All the while she looked over her shoulder, scanning for the exit. We both held our breath.

"Great, now put the money on the table," I said.

"OK. That's it? Can I get out of here now?" she said, as she backed away a couple of steps.

"No. There's one more thing you need to do," I said. Once again I used my "mommy-means-business" face. She froze. "Stay the f**k away from married men."

With my last scrap of dignity I lifted up M. and grabbed my soaked, ruined, designer bag. M.'s diarrhea dripped down into my shoes, oozing between my toes. My walk of shame was punctuated by the splosh, splosh, splosh of my slime filled shoes. I took three more steps. And then, still holding my child, I ran.

In many ways, I've never stopped.

minivan memoirs

by Dawn Meehan

At store. Told salesclerk I had six kids. She said, "Oh, how many grandkids do you have?" I hit her with my purse.

When I got pregnant with my first child 15 years ago, my husband and I agreed that I would quit my job to be a stay-at-home-mom (SAHM) to raise our child. I didn't realize, at the time, that SAHM actually stood for "Sit All Hours in Minivan." For example, yesterday I woke up and started an IV drip of coffee while my two oldest teenagers had a nutritious breakfast of leftover birthday cake. When they were ready for school (in other words, after Savannah made sure her cell phone was charged and after I had told Austin to brush his teeth 50,000 times) I loaded up all six kids in my mobile home (i.e. my van) and dropped the two oldest kids off at school.

I was still in my pajamas, hair uncombed, sans make-up for this little trip. I do this on purpose because I've found it to be an especially good motivational tool. For example, my kids know that if they don't clean up their rooms like they're supposed to do, I've been known to step out of the car in my jammies and call to the kids, "Buh-bye Snuggle Buns! Have a good day! Mommy loves you!" For some reason, this is amazingly embarrassing to teenagers.

After dropping off the two oldest kids, I ran home and took a shower while the four youngest kids spilled half a gallon of milk on the floor and crushed a box of cereal in between the couch cushions. I threw some towels over the river of milk and ushered everyone back into the van so I could take the two middle kids to school. I pulled up to the Kiss 'N Drive lane where I got behind the parent who, instead of kissing their kid and driving off, took 15 minutes to dig out lunch money, sign homework assignments, and have an in depth conversation about global politics with their second grader.

After dropping Jackson and Lexi off, I returned home, washed my kitchen floor, switched loads of laundry, checked my e-mail, and hopped back in my van so I could take my youngest daughter, Brooklyn, to her doctor's appointment. Of course, I had to wait the requisite four and a half hours before seeing the doctor, which made me late to meet my girlfriend for lunch. I rushed from the doctor's office to McDonald's where I forced my kids to eat half a fry before turning them loose on the playground where they ran around like rabid monkeys. Too soon it was time to take my son, Clay to preschool, so I carried the kids kicking and screaming and persuaded them to leave and get back in the van.

I unloaded my son at preschool, drove home to do more laundry, pay bills, and start dinner. There's some sort of time warp that happens when I take my kids to school. For some reason, time accelerates and in the matter of five minutes, it's time to pick them up again. I loaded the baby into the car, picked up the junior high kids, hit the preschool for my son, then cruised on to the grade school for the middle kids.

From there, I drove to Target because we were out of necessities like toilet paper, diaper wipes, chocolate, and wine. I got home just in time to throw some dinner at the kids before herding everyone into the van yet again for our evening activities. I was really proud of myself for managing to get some semblance of a balanced meal together because more often than not I end up feeding my kids fast food on the run during baseball season. I'm pretty sure if we were ever stranded in a snowstorm, we could survive off the orphan fries on the floor of the van for at least a month.

We finished dinner and I left the dirty dishes on the table while I dropped Savannah off at softball practice and sped carefully across town to get Austin to his baseball game in time. Meanwhile, my husband took Jackson to his hockey game. (We usually have to divide and conquer when the kids have activities on the same night. We take turns watching the different games.) I rushed back to get Savannah from practice and headed across town so I could see the end of Austin's game while Savannah checked out the eighth-grade boys.

When all the games were over, I headed home so I could clean up the mess from dinner while my husband gave the little kids baths. Just as I was about to sit down and relax for a minute, Jackson yelled from the kitchen, "Mom, we're out of milk!" I guess I should have wrung the milky paper towels out into the carton this morning, but since I didn't do that, I was stuck running back out once again. Oh well, my day just wouldn't be complete unless I'd made at least ten trips in my van. Tomorrow I'm taking the van in to have a refrigerator and a toilet installed behind the seats. Hey, if you can't beat 'em, join 'em.

do you know the muffin top

By Tracy Beckerman ★ Author of the syndicated humor column, *Lost in Suburbia*

Tracy Beckerman has eaten one too many chocolate footballs.

One morning while I was in my bathroom, I overheard my kids talking in the hall.

"Where's mom," asked my son. "We're gonna be late for school."

"She's in the bathroom putting on her make-up," replied my daughter.

"Why does she have to wear make-up?" asked my son.

"To cover up her zits and wrinkles," replied my daughter.

I grimaced at my reflection in the mirror.

"Besides, it's not her make-up that takes so long," said my daughter. "It's blow-drying her hair."

"Why does she have to blow-dry her hair?" asked my son.

"Because it's dull and lifeless," said my daughter.

"HELLLOOO! I CAN HEAR YOU, YOU KNOW!!!" I bellowed from behind my dull and lifeless locks and the ton of make-up I had applied to cover my zits and wrinkles.

This is when I realized why I had children: to systematically eradicate any vestige of a positive self-image I ever had.

Of course my kids always tell me how no one in the world can make a peanut butter and jelly sandwich like I can. They tell me how I give great hugs and what an awesome laundry-doer I am. They constantly tell me I am the greatest mommy in the world, which is certainly nice to hear. But what I really want is for them to think I am the most beautiful mommy on the planet . . . or at least on our block.

Not that I'm shallow or anything.

Then one day when my daughter and I were on the supermarket checkout line, she looked over at one of the gossip magazines and gasped.

"Hey mom, you look just like a movie star," she exclaimed.

"Wow," I thought, "A movie star! My daughter really does think I'm beautiful!"

I joyfully glanced down to where she was pointing and saw a picture of a dimpled backside under a headline that screamed, "Stars with Cellulite."

Mission accomplished: Self-image eradicated.

Even though my days of short-shorts or even not-so-short-shorts were behind me, I decided motherhood was not going to keep me from being cute and cool. I had been cute and cool once and I was determined to get it back. I didn't know that I would ever get back into my pre-mom jeans, but I was OK with being cute and cool with a slightly larger backside than I had before.

Still, it was clear that the first issue I had to tackle was that stubborn post-baby weight. Contrary to popular opinion, chasing toddlers around the house does not burn off the weight you gain when you're pregnant. Actually, it might work if not for the mac-and-cheese I consistently finished off my toddler's plate. So, for a long time post-pregnancy I found myself sporting what is known in mommy circles as a Baby Belly. Having already had the baby, it is clear that there is, obviously, no baby in the Baby Belly. It is the belly caused by having HAD the baby.

There are some women who lose their Baby Belly about three months after giving birth. Then there's me. I had my Baby Belly right up until I got pregnant with my second child and got so attached to it, I kept it until the kids were 9 and 11, at which point you don't call it a Baby Belly anymore, you just simply call it FAT.

Clearly, the time had come to join a gym and declare war on the Baby Belly.

"OK ladies, let's grab some weights and work on those Bat Wings," said my Amazon fitness instructor, Betty Biceps, on the first day of my "Butts and Guts" class.

"I thought we were working on our Baby Belly," I said.

"We'll do the Baby Belly after the Bat Wings," she explained.

"And what are the Bat Wings," I asked naively.

"That's the fat under your arms," she said. The roomful of upper arm-challenged women flapped the loose skin under their triceps to demonstrate.

"Oh, wait," said Betty. "I forgot. Before we do the Bat Wings, we need to work on our Muffin Tops."

I stared blankly.

"That's the fat around your middle that rolls over the top of your jeans and makes your waist look like a muffin," she explained. I pinched my Muffin Top. I think it was a corn muffin.

We started doing some jumping jacks until I was afraid we would take flight with our Bat Wings.

"If you add a lunge here, it will also help with your Banana Folds," Betty shouted over the din of women jumping.

"And the Banana Folds are ..." I queried.

"The band of fat on the back of your legs just below your derriere," she yelled.

Looking in the mirror, I wondered what other food groups had been designated for some roll of fat on my body.

Finally, I stopped lunging and with my Baby Belly, my Bat Wings, my Muffin Top and my Banana Folds, I rolled up my yoga mat and walked to the door.

"Hey, where are you going," called Betty.

"I'm going to get some breakfast," I said. "All this talk about muffins and bananas is making me hungry."

Realizing that exercise alone was not going to get the baby weight off, I decided to embark on a sensible diet. However with so many diets out there, I wasn't sure which one to try. I thought about calling a mom-friend of mine for advice. She's been trying to lose the same ten pounds for ten years. She thinks that sensible eating is the key to weight loss... for other people. She's tried every new diet known to woman. She's done the Bloomingdale's Diet, Scarsdale Diet, and Sugarbusters. She's eaten only beets for one week and only lima beans for the next. Actually, I think that one was called the Disgusting Vegetables Diet. She's taken these mystery herbal pills that she ordered online that have since been banned in this country after two dozen people grew something like an extra liver from taking them. She owns a Thigh Master, a Butt Buster, and this stuff that looks like cellophane that she wraps around her thighs with this special cream underneath that's supposed to melt away the cellulite. Not only did it not melt the fat, it actually increased the hair growth on her upper thighs. So now, each summer she has to diet as well as have her legs waxed hourly.

Currently, she's on an ultra-high protein diet, eats nothing but steak and eggs and has a cholesterol count so high that Lipitor wants to pay HER to take their drugs. Whenever spring rolls around and I tell her I need to lose weight, she tries to recruit me into her Fad Diet Cult. However, I'd rather stay inside for the summer, than subject myself to a season of lima beans and hairy thighs, so I politely decline.

Ultimately I went on a little-known but effective regimen called the "Stop Eating the Kids' Leftovers off Their Plates," diet. Many weeks of eating rabbit food and doing bat wing-shrinking exercises later, I finally decided I had taken enough wiggle out of my jiggly parts to try on a bathing suit. Since no one had yet invented a bathing suit that covers you from your neck to your knees, I opted for one of those "Miracle Suits," and then prayed for one as I squeezed my body into it. I looked in my funhouse skinny mirror that I bought from an amusement park supply store for just this purpose and decided I couldn't be objective about my own bathing suit-worthiness.

"How do I look in this bathing suit?" I asked my husband

He looked at me over the top of the *Sports Illustrated* Swimsuit Issue he was reading. "Has any husband ever in the history of the world been stupid enough to answer that question?"

"Seriously, how do I look?" I asked again.

"Honey, you always look beautiful to me," he replied lovingly.

"You're not answering my question."

"Hmm, I think it looks like rain," he said glancing out the window.

"Hmmmph!" I stomped out of the room and downstairs to where the kids were watching TV. I knew my kids would be brutally honest so I decided to model my suit for them.

"Hey guys, how do you like this bathing suit?"

They kept watching TV.

"I said, how do I look in this bathing suit?" I repeated loudly.

My daughter finally glanced over. "You have extra butt hanging out the back," she said definitively and turned back to the TV.

Without batting an eye, I picked up the phone and called my diet friend.

"Exactly how much thigh hair are we talking about, really?"

fire trucks are dangerous

By Issa M. Mas ★ Single Mama NYC

Ran out of milk. Thought soy formula in my coffee might work instead. Ladies, please, don't EVER do that . . . shudder.

As a single mom, I have to get a whole lot done on my own. I've been single since my second month of pregnancy, so by now I'm usually pretty good at managing everything. Once I stopped working in corporate America and became a freelance writer and blogger I actually found myself multitasking even more, and although I have a fabulous sitter a couple of days a week, I still tend to juggle quite a bit by myself, and things can get, well . . . interesting.

A couple of months ago, I was all set to interview the headmistress of an upscale private school in New York City for my website. The article was supposed to cover the new initiative this school was undertaking in attempts to diversify their student body. To accomplish this directive, they had allotted spots in every grade to be held for students from lower income families. I, also, truth be told, wanted to get in good standing with her because I loved the idea of my son being able to attend such an exclusive preschool.

Sure, he was only 19 months old at the time, but in New York City, if you want to get your child into a really good preschool, you pretty much have to register them while they're in utero. So, this was my big chance to not only land a great story for my single parenting site, but to perhaps get my son into a top-notch school I couldn't really afford.

On the day I was scheduled to interview the headmistress, my son's sitter was going to watch him for the day. That morning, as I was getting Theo dressed to drop him off at the sitter's house, she called me sounding hoarse and extremely congested. Great. Just great. The interview was in less than an hour, and there was no one else available to watch my kid.

OK, no big deal. I decided to simply set him up with my guilt-laden stand-by—Jack's Big Music Show on On Demand. I really can't stand plopping my kid down in front of the television and using it as a babysitter, but sometimes it is an absolute necessity. I would have the matted hair, filthy skin, tattered clothes and rotted teeth of a Black Plague-era peasant if it weren't for the Godsend that is Jack's Big Music Show on On Demand. So, I went over to the television and turned it on to the Noggin On Demand channel and . . . nothing. Just a black screen. What?!? I didn't understand what was happening, so I changed it to a different On Demand channel, and up popped the program menu for that channel. OK, so my television was working. Good. I turned it back to the Noggin On Demand channel, and NOTHING. DEAR GOD IN HEAVEN, WHY??? "Please don't do this to me," I actually started begging God. "I can't get on this call with Theo at home without that show holding his attention. He'll be clamoring for my attention every two and a half minutes, and if I don't respond immediately, his whining may attract a pack a rabid dogs. Please God, if you ever loved me, please make the channel come back."

Nothing.

So, now, not only was I panicking about how this extremely important phone interview would go while my toddler was at home with me, but I had incontrovertible proof that God has indeed never loved me. Wonderful.

The time was quickly approaching for me to make my call to the headmistress, so I started to really panic. Theo, of course, smelled my fear, as all children/wild animals do, and began to act even more unruly than usual. He yanked his farm animals out of his little tractor trailer and screamed their respective sounds as he flung them across the room. "MOOOO," he bellowed, as the cow sailed through the air and careened into the living room wall. "BAAAA," went the sheep, as it landed with a thud.

God had clearly abandoned me. I made a mental note to purchase a goat and make the appropriate sacrifice at some point that evening.

With five minutes left until call time, I sat Theo down with every single vehicle he had and tried to get him to calm down. He had his tractor (sans animals), his Leap Frog bus, his soft toddler Tonka Trucks, his ambulance, and his fire truck. He absolutely loves fire trucks—whenever we see them on the street he gets excited and points and shouts out what they are. Here's the thing though: although he can usually say the word Truck with no problem, the "F" in Fire Truck throws him off and he ends up saying "Fire F**k"—usually at the top of his lungs. At first it was amusing, but it had somehow gotten increasingly less so as people would whip their heads over in our direction in disbelief at what they thought they just heard that adorable little boy say.

OK, so, I set him up with his vehicles, knowing it could feasibly buy me at least ten minutes of uninterrupted time, and I didn't really expect the interview to last more than ten to fifteen minutes anyway, as I figured her answers to my questions would be fairly succinct. Theo was playing quietly with his vehicles, and I gathered up the courage to make the call, all the while praying to God (who currently may or may not have been ticked off at me for some unknown reason), that all would go well on the call. The headmistress picked up immediately; we exchanged greetings, and then got right down to the interview. Unsurprisingly, the headmistress was quite terse in her answers. She also didn't seem the least bit interested in actually having lower-income children mixing in with her elite clientele, but made it very clear that this was what the Board wanted, and so she was faithfully following their directives. She said that she didn't have the slightest notion as to where she would find this "lower-class clientele," and thanked me for the opportunity to reach my demographic. At this point, I couldn't stand this woman, but the school was in the top three ranking of all private schools in Manhattan, so I was laser-focused on using this call as a means to get the best education possible for my son.

It was at that moment that my son came tearing over to me pointing at the living room window. My apartment is in the front of the building facing the street, and you can unfortunately hear most of the sounds on the street below, as we are only on the second floor. A fire truck was roaring down our street (further evidence of God's wrath set upon me), and Theo was screaming, "Fire F**K! Fire F**K!"

Mortified, I tried shooing him away before he got to me; I pushed him gently back towards his play area once he arrived, but of course, he wanted verbal acknowledgment that I had heard him. "FIRE F**K! FIRE F**K!!!" he shouted in my face.

Dear God, what have I done to offend Thee???

I tried wrapping things up with the headmistress and asked her if it would be alright to e-mail any follow-up questions, to which she replied yes. Relieved, I was about to thank her for her time and get off of the phone when Theo came back over with his own fire truck in his hands and said, "Fire F**K, Mama! FIRE F**K!"

"I see that you have your hands full at present; I shall leave you to it then," Miss Snooty von Headmistress said, disdainfully, and hung up.

"Oh, Truck her," I thought. I don't want Theo in a school like that anyway.

the tooth fairy, the torah, and me

By Nancy Friedman ★ From Hip to Housewife

Nancy Friedman is bowling. Yes, bowling. Raining. Weekend. Kids. Desperate.

It's Rosh Hashanah, the day most Jews think of as among the most holy of the year. The day you confess your sins: gossiping, yelling at your kids, lying about your weight. It's the day that determines whether or not you'll be inscribed into the Book of Life, or doomed forever. But I'm not prostrating myself, admitting to my sins of gluttony, pride, excessive sarcasm, or intense dislike of size-two women who insist they eat French fries. Nope. I'm not praying. I'm not standing up and sitting down and standing up and sitting down. I'm in a hotel party room listening to my Rabbi telling a story in which he refers to his car's GPS as an automotive dominatrix. Still, it is Rosh Hashanah, and I am a Jewish mother, so here I am.

I was raised a militantly secular Jew, a red diaper baby, complete with a Workman's Circle school where I studied Jewish culture in a Church basement on Saturday mornings. In lieu of Hebrew, I learned Yiddish. (Incredibly valuable in getting discounts on cameras in midtown Manhattan.) In lieu of a Bat Mitzvah, I wrote a "scholarly" paper on the Maranos of South America. (Incredibly valuable for . . . well, not so valuable.) I learned folk dancing; I read stories by Sholem Aleichem and I. B. Singer. I sang songs about the Warsaw Ghetto uprising, the struggle of the worker against authority, and the need to fight against oppression. And then I went back to my seven-bedroom house with live-in help.

Those weekly three hour sessions of socialist camaraderie may have had nothing whatsoever to do with the rest of my life, but they gave me if not religion, then a religious fervor for righteous behavior, good works, and fairness. Even amidst all that privilege, every Saturday, I was reminded of what really mattered. And I associated that meaning with Judaism.

Then I went off to college, and suddenly my parents decided it was time to join a synagogue. Maybe it was the sight of me anointing the feet of my born-again boyfriend that made them change gears, maybe it was the fact that my militantly a-religious grandmother had died so there was no one to scoff at my mother trying out traditional religion. Whatever the reason, there I was, eighteen years old, at my first High Holy Day service standing up and sitting down with the rest of them.

The stories told in that service were the traditional Rosh Hashanah Torah readings which then, I knew only vaguely, but in the years to come, I would learn to tune out with ease. The story I remember best is the one where God asks

Abraham to prove his devotion by sacrificing his son, Isaac to him. With an axe! Then, just as Abraham is about to lower that axe, God steps in and tells Abraham Ha! Ha! It had just been a test. Like the old saying goes: It's all well and good until somebody loses a son!

What? My only exposure to synagogue had been at friends' Bar Mitzvahs. Where was the DJ throwing "Amy's Big Day" t-shirts at us? Where were the kvelling grandparents? The feuding divorced couple? Why wasn't there an ice-sculpture depicting the onset of puberty? I hadn't counted on stories of divine intervention, of bible stories that would fit right in to an episode of Jerry Springer. To me, Judaism was all about folk songs, and dancing, and eating so much that the indigestion lasted for days. At that first service, I endured incomprehensible Hebrew, an interminable sermon, and an even more endless plea for cash. My parent's decision to send me to a secular Jewish school was looking pretty good.

Then I had my own children. What should I do for them? As if my own Jewish upbringing weren't unorthodox enough, my husband was raised in an orthodox synagogue, but ate bacon cheeseburgers at home. We both wanted our kids to feel like they were part of the Jewish community without making ourselves feel like total hypocrites. (Did I mention the bacon cheeseburger?)

And that's how I ended up sitting with my family in a secular Jewish congregation at the Marriott in lower Manhattan. As I looked around the room at the aggressively un-chic crowd an appliquéd sweater here, an oversized Batik muumuu there, a truly horrendous assortment of shoes, and an amazing amount of hair so frizzy one would think an electric current were running through the room, I thought to myself: these are my people. We are Humanistic Jews: all the guilt, all the lox and cream cheese, all the self-hatred and pride, and none of the hocus pocus.

Humanistic Jews believe we don't need a supernatural authority to be Jewish. We have our traditions, our culture. We have Woody Allen and Mel Brooks. We have history; we have our resentment and paranoia. We have an uncanny ability to be victimized. Who needs that Abraham and Isaac stuff?

Yet here I am, I, sitting in a hotel ballroom with a bunch of left-wing Jews celebrating what most other Jews consider the holiest day of the year. Why? Because of the Tooth Fairy.

The last time my daughter, Rachel, lost a tooth, the Tooth Fairy "forgot to come."

"The Tooth Fairy NEVER CAME!!!" Rachel sobbed as she burst into our room that morning. "And I know what that means, you're the Tooth Fairy and you forgot."

If I were a fundamentalist Christian I would have donned a hair shirt and whipped myself silly. But I am a Jew, so I will just feel guilty forever. Until that very moment, I would have bet the farm (OK, we live in Manhattan—I would have bet the coveted storage bin in the basement) that my daughter didn't really believe in the Tooth Fairy, that she was choosing to believe. Like how I believe every single commercial about face cream. Intellectually, I know they're not going to visibly fade my dark spots, improve the appearance of fine lines, or heighten elasticity by 70%, but every time they come out with something new, I fall for it. My medicine chest is a paean to face-fads past ... but I digress.

Clearly, my daughter had believed. She was hysterical. My son offered this reassuring gem: "Oh come on. The Tooth Fairy is like Santa Claus," he said. "It's just made up."

My daughter looked stricken. "Mommy, is it true? Is the Tooth Fairy made up? Like Santa Claus?"

Now I had a problem. My husband and I don't want our kids to believe in Santa Claus the commercialism, the materialism, the fact that if they believed they'd feel terrible that he doesn't come to our house. But the Tooth Fairy? She's about the wondrous, dare I say miraculous, process of growing up.

"OK," I said, I'll tell you the truth." And then I lied. "The first time, the Tooth Fairy really does come. But after that, she tries to get to every child who loses a tooth, but she just doesn't have enough magic. So she counts on parents to check to see if she's left a present. And last night, Daddy and I forgot to check."

And just like that, she believed again.

I am moved at the ability of faith to supersede all reason. I am amazed by my own daughter's ability to understand and forgive. And I realize I didn't lie to my daughter, because there is a magical fairy-like quality to that first lost tooth. The Tooth Fairy matters. And not just because of the cash. The Tooth Fairy is part of the ritual of childhood. She is only the vehicle of the myth, not the truth of it. I don't need to believe something to see the truth in it. The truth is, the myth of the Tooth Fairy soothes the pain of a losing a tooth, the fear of growing older, the embarrassment of having two front teeth way too big for your face . . . or of not having them at all for a while. The Tooth Fairy is part of the mythical time we call childhood.

That's why I drag my kids to nontheist Sunday school. That's why we light candles on Friday night and then eat pork chops. Because of the Tooth Fairy. Because even if I don't believe in some bearded dude directing everything from on high, even if I don't believe in the Tooth Fairy herself, I believe there's magic in all that ritual.

And who is to say where the magic may lie? In the stories of Rosh Hashanah? In the ritual of lighting candles? Of blessing the wine? Of complaining that the soup isn't hot enough, the apartment not clean enough, the girl not good enough for our only son. And if there isn't any magic, how do you explain anyone liking gefilte fish?

The night of my Tooth Fairy fiasco, as I tucked my daughter in, I felt something under her pillow. It was a note: "Dear Tooth Fairy," it read, "I'm sorry I didn't believe in you. I know you're very busy. Love, Rachel." If that's not magic, what is?

busy

by Abby Pecoriello ★ Crafty Mama

Too harried to Tweet.

I couldn't pick one harried moment because my whole life is like a whole freaking harried-a-thon.

Also, I can't think of one harried moment because I'm not such a great moment-rememberer. Most embarrassing moment? Proudest moment? Happiest moment? I got no clue!

Anyhoo ... Back to me being harried.

I'm harried. I'm hairy. I'm married. I'm merry. (You know my best friend from college, Marla, who is from Michigan thinks that MARRY, MERRY, and MARY are all pronounced the same: MARY?)

But that all really has nothing to do with me being busy, does it?

OK.

I will now officially start my essay!

Harried Abby. Take Two.

I am harried. My parents are harried. It's in the Miller blood.

Everyone in my family loves to make themselves way, way busier than they really have to be!

Instead of a simple trip to the mall for those cheap Madonna rubber bracelets ... my mom and dad schlepped me all over New Jersey from auto part shop to auto part shop to get me a whole rubbery FREE collection of them. They were cute, but they sort of smelled!

My parents couldn't just get their gas at a gas station? Nope! My dad researched and researched and then bought a diesel pump and put it in the backyard ... in a shed that he and my brothers built. They busied themselves for months and months making it ... so they wouldn't have to go to freaking EXXON once a week!

WHAT?

My childhood Thanksgivings were not at a family table with turkey and taters. No! We spent most of our Thanksgivings schlepping around Europe (cause my mom, pre-Expedia, got super cheap tickets by busying herself calling every airline, every day). We'd run around for four days crazily trying to see every single church on the map. And we're JEWISH!

My whole life my parents have made their lives busier than they really were ... and they still do it! And now I totally do it too!

I can't just go to work 9 to 5 like a sane person. No! I have to obsessively work all day long ... in my office ... on my Blackberry ... on the subway ... on my computer at home ... on the toilet (I admit it, I sometimes e-mail on the potty! Sorry!).

I have to respond to every e-mail I get ... even if it's with a "thanks!" or "got it!" or "yay!" (But NEVER a LOL. I don't LOL. I can't. I dunno why, I just can't. I prefer hehe.)

I can't just get someone a gift off their baby registry. Why would I easily get them what they've asked for ... when I could stay up until one in the morning making them delicious little personalized T-shirts with pictures of Miss Piggy or David Hasselhoff on them! Or personalizing a diaper wipe box for them by blinging it out with their baby's name! ****ELLA!*****

RIDIC!

I can't just celebrate birthdays and holidays with my extended fam! Goodness no! I need to go to their school plays and piano recitals and soccer games and birthday parties and half-birthday parties (for real) and going-to-sleep-away-camp parties and even their I-just-got-my-braces-off parties! We had one for Justin.

It was really good. There were a LOT of gummy bears!

NOOOOOOO JOKE!

And my kids ... FORGET ABOUT IT! It's a harried-palooza!

I can't just do puzzles with them! I need to bust out my linoleum knife so I can make home made stamps with them, or help them transform a little IKEA egg chair into a space ship with three rolls of aluminum foil and a few colanders, or help choreograph and costume them for their Tuesday night living room performance of *CATS* ("I'd see it again and again!").

I can't just have a birthday party for them at Little Gym, Mini Chefs, or Bounce U! No, silly! I have to brainstorm a theme, handmake a special invite, and then dream up the games, the cake, the costumes, and BE the entertainment ... in my personally transformed playroom.

I can't just chillax on the weekends! Are you serious?! We go to the diner, then the playground, then the children's museum, then to the dollar store on 32nd street, then for ice cream at YOLATO (well, it's not really ice cream it's yogurt-gelato), then to Cayla's for a playdate, and then to my niece's just to top off the day!

I always make everything busier and crazier and more ridiculous than it needs to be. And you know what? I LOVE IT! It totally keeps me on my toes. Ugh. My toes. I wore sandals the other day and I think I have a corn on my toe. I don't really know what a corn is, but I know what I got isn't a bunion or a wart . . . so I'm thinking corn. I'm gonna get those little circle Band-Aids for it.

I digress. I just can't have downtime. I hate it. And if I have it, I find something to do! And make it more complicated and silly than it has to be!

Of course this drives my husband ABSOLUTELY NUTS! (All the more reason to do it, right?) But this is coming from the guy who wants a television so he hops across the street to get it at BestBuy. BESTBUY! Hello, WORST BUY!

The way you get a television is that you call my brother, Wayne Miller, and have him help you scour the Internet for the best prices and all the coupon codes and rebates and then get that television from some website that's hosted in East Chipipi, Indiana but . . . of course, has FREE SHIPPING!

I admit it . . .

I love being harried. My favorite movie is *When Harried Met Sally*. I read all of the Harried Potter books! I even played Harried-et Tubman in my fifth grade play! (I know, I'm white, but I went to a wonderfully liberal elementary school!)

Harried, harried, harried is just my way of life.

That said, I totally need a nap!

the traditional new york city pedicure

by Jenny Baitch Isenman ★ Suburban Jungle

I can't decide between "After Sex" or "Three Bottles of Whine."

So I am finally getting a long-overdue pedicure. This current span has been about two months or 68 days, but who's counting? I like to let the nails grow unattractively long in the true spirit of martyrdom. Then I wear sandals and constantly draw attention to how badly I need a pedicure, by saying things like, "How badly do I need a pedicure?"

The trick is to go as infrequently as possible and only surrender when your nails split and a jagged edge pulls threads in your sheets, thereby making a 3 a.m. roll over feel like chewing on metal. Most importantly, do not, under any circumstance, remove the polish. This way you have undeniable proof of your hectic schedule. It implies that your "me time" is so sparse that you don't even have enough to simply wet a cotton ball.

Today I arrived with the red so far at the tip it looked as if I was starting a new trend in French pedicures. Sarabeth, whose real name is Choi Jae Hua or Yi Hae-Won or something else I can't pronounce, looks at my feet with a "Tsk." "I know it's been a long time," I say with the joy of squeezing in one last sympathizer. Then she looks up at me and asks if I am aware there is a Pokémon sticker on the bottom of my foot. "Oh, my son was looking for that. If only it were so easy to find my keys." She then asks if it's OK to remove it. "Well if you can't work around it." I'm not sure if she can hear me; my chair is set on high-multifunction-ten. Its "Human Hand" technology is violently knocking me out of my seat while it heats my tush, vibrates my thighs, froths milk for my cappuccino, and sorts my mail.

I lie, well, shimmy back trying to enjoy my favorite part, the massage. I can't seem to relax. I am so keenly aware of every leftover scrub granule that is kneaded into my legs. Worse, I can sense her daydreaming of the family she's left behind and I'm sure she's totally resenting me for not shaving, detesting America for making her touch feet, and cursing her boss for making today "$20 Tuesday." I finally start to relax as she coincidentally realizes she has massaged long enough. She halts to do the required Korean calf knocking, which she follows with the "Ten-Toe-Pop" event. She's seems let down when she can't get a good snap out of the last two toes (not unlike that annoying handshake of the mid-nineties).

"OK, pick you color" she says pointing to the wall. I can't decide between "After Sex" or a hue one shade darker,

"Three Bottles of Whine." I don't understand why all the colors are sexual innuendos. In the end I go with "Popped Cherry," which is a medium shade of . . . well, you get the picture. I spend most of the polish application staring at the tranquil paintings of nude women relaxing on furniture. The woman in the painting across from me appears to be giving herself a breast exam on a plush sofa.

I decided to heighten my relaxation by purchasing a ten minute massage. I swiftly wriggle myself into the pretzel seat after viewing a short video demonstration by Cirque Du Soleil. Then she literally beats the tension out of me. "Excuse me Sarabeth, that knot you're trying to knead out, I think that's bone." She ignores me, as she does not recognize the sound of her own name. No matter, she manages to pummel it smooth regardless. Then she grabs my wrists, pulls my arms back and relentlessly yanks trying to crack my shoulder blades. She ends with vigorous karate chops to the back of my neck. Sarabeth then signals someone, and an EMT rushes in with the Jaws of Life to free me from the chair. I walk away totally relaxed, one arm carelessly dangling from the socket. No worries. I'm sure it's nothing a good orthopedist can't fix. Why do my attempts at tension release always seem to stress me out?

fear of flying

by Sara Fisher ★ Self Made Mom

The man in the paint store just asked me how many weeks I had left, and when I said 7, he said, "boy, there's a big one in there."

I'm a cool flyer. In fact, I'm a super cool flyer. I started flying solo at a young age. I can actually remember a time when airport security guards didn't dress up in faux-authoritative uniforms and do strip searches on your toiletries.

Flying doesn't rattle me. I flew two weeks after 9/11. I've been the last plane to land in a violent snowstorm. I've slept overnight in terminals in foreign countries. I've been double-booked, cancelled, diverted, rerouted, circled, refueled, de-iced, de-planed, and just about everything in between.

Flying doesn't rattle me. Except when I have to fly with my son. Because really, I can think of nothing that scares me more than being trapped in a hot, stuffy, bumpy, dirty, and smelly confined space with a toddler with nothing but a wing (or two), a prayer, and limited computer/DVD/iPod battery life.

Before my son was born, I had these grand plans of how I'd make him the consummate traveler. Start him at a young age! Let him watch whatever he likes! Bribe him with treats! Dose him with Benadryl!

What I've come to realize is this: when it comes to flying, practice does not make perfect. I feel grateful nowadays if I can make it through a solo flight with my son without evident stains on my clothes and a diaper bag that doesn't look as if it's been ransacked by the TSA.

But in the beginning of our travels together, I got a little too confident about flying with a child. I had just come off a successful jaunt from Chicago to my hometown of Detroit. Successful meaning that I was able to finish ten pages of an issue of *Us Weekly* before the pilot said I had to turn off our electronic devices. (The words I dread most hearing on an airplane next to, "fasten your seat belts, it's going to get bumpy.") All I needed was a smooth return flight and bingo! I would have survived the first 18 months of my son's life without one of those airplane horror stories.

I should have known not to try to fly to O'Hare at rush hour with the forecast calling for the "Blizzard of 2008."

I figured, how bad could it be? The maximum flying time between Detroit and Chicago is around 45 minutes. By the time you go up, it's time to come down. But flying in the Midwest in January is never without its challenges. We incurred delay after delay. (Why is it so hard to fly in the snow? Doesn't the hot jet fuel just melt it all?) We got on the plane, we got off. We got on again. We found the last remaining flight attendant on duty for United Airlines whose flying hours had not exceeded his daily limit. We gave him a standing ovation. We were over five hours delayed. We needed to get home.

We took our seats. We took off. I looked over at my beautiful, well-behaved boy, who at this point was up three hours past his designated bedtime. His very rigid (I read sleep books like they were the Bible) bedtime.

Then we landed again. But it was far too soon. I know that landing pattern over O'Hare well. Where you go way out past the airport only to circle back again. Otherwise known as the point in time where everyone on the plane makes the mad dash for their cell phones. This time, however, the airport didn't look familiar. The runway felt shorter, and well, people didn't seem all that eager to call their loved ones. It couldn't be Chicago.

It wasn't.

"Ladies and gentleman," the captain, who must have drank at least four Red Bulls at this point to stay awake because we were all asleep, said, "Uh, we had to make a diversion in Grand Rapids to refuel."

Refuel? Between Detroit and Chicago? It couldn't be. This is the trip they take those really small, don't-hit-your-head-on-the-door-on-the-way-out planes. Easy breezy.

But here we were, in a blizzard, refueling a Boeing 757 in Grand Rapids, Michigan. A mere two and a half hour drive from my house. I could have taken a dogsled at this point and gotten home faster.

I was tempted to get off the plane through the emergency exit. I was tempted to take the gentlemanly flight attendant who allowed us to take the flight in the first place by the throat and say, "You do realize I WILL BE USING YOUR SHIRT to diaper my child if we don't get out of here soon. Don't you?"

There's the rub. I had enough supplies to get me to CHICAGO. Not Cairo.

But no, we didn't deplane, we didn't drive, and I never got my dogsled. We waited and finally arrived at our destination at midnight, a 10-hour trip for a 45 minute flight.

I thought this was bad, but I hadn't known the half of it. Even though we arrived at our destination far past our scheduled arrival time, tired, disheveled, hungry, and stiff-necked, we were dry and still had all of our original clothes on.

I'll explain.

Flying is like the newborn phase of child rearing. No matter how bad of an experience you have, you always get back on that plane. It's like someone wipes out every short-term memory cell of every flight you take and every child you have. Otherwise we'd all have one kid and drive everywhere we go.

So while the Blizzard of 2008 flight was the flight from hell, it didn't deter me from ever flying again with my child. I have those friends, mind you. The ones who have one bad trip with a two-year-old and then decide never to go anywhere again with their children until they're teenagers.

But not me. I got right back up on that horse, er, plane again. And again. When free babysitting, as in Nana and Papa, live out of state, you'll do almost anything to get some.

Thus, I endured puke. Puke on a plane. I can assure you it's worse than snakes.

I should have seen the telltale signs as we were landing. An otherwise docile child moaning in agony, crying, holding his stomach, pointing to his mouth. A clueless mother asking what's wrong. It's too late at that point. That was the good news. I didn't see it coming, so I couldn't panic and get all grossed out.

The bad news was that I couldn't contain the puke. I never knew how hard it was to find that sick bag until I really needed it. Because when you really need it, it's usually not there. Or it's there, but it's crammed between the sticky sheets of the SkyMall catalog and someone's used gum and as such, rendered completely useless.

I've also learned that when bodily fluids go flying when a plane is landing, it's quite hard to summon the help you need. All you get are lots of sympathetic (and grossed out) stares from others in the rows next to you. Of course, since I saw none of the signs, I was ill prepared.

But my maternal instincts kicked in. No more wipes? Fine, that shirt will do. No paper towel, garbage bag, or water? Ah! The SkyMall catalog finally had a good use. By the time the flight attendants could get out of their seats and throw some napkins my way I had a naked, screaming toddler on my lap and the world's most disgusting airplane seat next to me.

It was all I could do to get off the plane. We peeled out fast. I didn't need those people sitting behind me to find out what had happened. But I had no clothes. No, not for me, for him. My poor little man had ruined all of his possessions

No matter, I thought. If taking your kids out half-naked in public is good enough for Britney, well, it's good enough for me. So we rolled Spears-style through the airport to baggage claim where I fell defeated into my husband's arms.

Sometimes, even when we try to overcome our fears, they still manage to bite us in the ass or upchuck all over us. But when you're a mom, where there's a will, there's a way. Or there's always saving up for that private jet.

40th birthday

By Eden Pontz ★ NYC Moms Blog

Like most people, I put my pants on one leg at a time. But today, I couldn't find my pants!

I wanted my 40th birthday to pass by much like an F-117 Stealth fighter off the radar. So, when my husband mentioned Wednesday morning, my birthday, that he was hoping I could leave work by 6 p.m. so we could go out (I typically work much later), I was nervous about what he'd planned, and even more so, how I'd break free by that time.

"What exactly did you have in mind?" I inquired.

"Nothing big, I just thought we could celebrate," he said coyly.

Wait. He's never coy. Cue the spy music in my head. Oh, I hope he's not planned a surprise party.

Wait, maybe it would be cool to have a surprise party! But on a Wednesday? Then again, maybe he's thinking that I'd never think, that he'd think, about having a surprise party in the middle of the week! Well, regardless of what we'd be doing, I knew I'd have to burn some rubber to make it home by that time.

It was my day to get my daughter, Jade, to school, and I knew this supposedly simplistic task could be precedent-setting as to how the rest of my day would go, so I'd need to be prepared to employ any tactics necessary to keep things moving. Too bad those scientists at CERN haven't discovered the key to time and space travel yet. How convenient would it be to have a giant particle accelerator in our study, allowing me to zap myself and my kid over to the Kiddie Korner Pre-K following breakfast?

"Time to get dressed honey! Hurry!" I yelled to Jade as I emerged from the shower, noticing a blemish on my chin. There's something so unjust about having to endure acne on your 40th birthday knowing that likely, the only real cure for your pimple is menopause.

"Just a minute Mommy! I'm tucking in Sweet Lilly!" my daughter yelled back from her bedroom. Jade was four and had just recently mastered the art of dressing herself from top to bottom. She'd also mastered the art of time procrastination, taught, of course, by the master, her mother. In our house, there are many different time valuations. There's us running on football time (one minute = ten), basketball time (one minute = five), soccer time (one minute = one)—annoyingly this is the time my husband usually runs on—and then there's Mom time, in which one minute = anything ranging from 15 minutes on upward, depending on whether I've gotten hold of my Blackberry, or I'm showering, or packing for a trip—you get the idea. Again, that time travel would be handy.

So when my daughter cried, "One minute" from her bedroom, I was certain she was nowhere near starting to get herself dressed. I hastened my bathroom primping, which in light of the circumstances, allowed for some zit cream, hair brushing, and a dollop of hair gel, to fight the impending frizz-filled day.

I sped down the hall to my bedroom and threw on my standard work-fare black pants, black top, black socks, and some more black stuff to round out the outfit. And then I sprinted back down the hall to my daughter's room.

"Mommyyyy!!" she cried as she looked at me. And then she really began crying. Sobbing. Uncontrollably.

"Pumpkin, what's wrong?" I asked, unavoidably glancing at the large, iridescent numbers of the clock on her windowsill. More tears burst forth from her blue eyes.

"Sweetie pie, I can't help you until you tell me what's wrong."

"You . . . you . . . you GOT DRESSED BEFORE ME!" she screamed violently.

Did I mention that coincidentally at the very same time Jade mastered her ability to procrastinate, she also went on a bender about the need to be first at anything and everything? From finishing smoothies, to brushing her teeth, to getting ready for bed—nothing was immune to her "quest for firstness."

"But honey, I said you needed to hurry, and I . . . "

"I'm not getting dressed until you get UNDRESSED!"

I did a perfunctory weighing of my options. And I saw her darn clock ticking quickly forward. And then, I dropped my trousers, took off my shirt, and said, "OK, now please, get dressed."

"But you still have your socks, and underwear and bah-wah on," she sniffed.

She folded her hands across her chest and waited. I

rolled my eyes, sighed, and off came my bra, my socks, and finally my underwear. She gave me a satisfied nod, and then, ever so precisely, stepped over to her bureau to pick out her clothes. I flashed forward in my mind thinking that this ugly scene would somehow morph and variations would play out many times once she hit her teens. Or her tweens. Or kindergarten. Flash back to reality, and I noticed her fumbling through some out of season clothes. How did she find those? I'd hidden them in the back of the dresser at the very bottom of the pile! She was like a pig honing in on truffles, only the prize was her black, short-sleeved, pink-sequined "Hello Kitty" shirt. I could see where this was headed, and I wasn't about to go there, because at this rate, if we didn't get a move on, school would be letting out by the time we arrived.

"Sweets, you can wear Hello Kitty" if you put a long sleeved shirt underneath." Miraculously, she complied and, somehow, managed to get the rest of her clothes on while taking ONLY another 23 minutes. I sat on her bed, grabbed her fuzzy Dora blanket (the one that was a present), tried to stay warm, tapped my foot, checked the clock, drummed my fingers on my knee, and tried my best not to sigh. The moment she finished, I whipped my clothes back on at breakneck speed.

Together we zoomed into the kitchen, while I bastardized aloud, the words made famous by Alice in Wonderland's white rabbit, "We're late, we're late, for a very important date! No time to stand around and cry, we're late, we're late, we're late!" As I saw the stovetop clock, I rummaged for something Jade could eat along the preschool route. No time for a proper sit-down breakfast today! "Sweets for my sweet?" I asked as I handed her a chocolate brownie cliff bar, and hoped that my husband didn't emerge to see my choice. Jade eagerly took the bar and gobbled it down. At least something inspired some hustle from her!

I scrambled to get her lunch and backpack together and made a quick bathroom pit stop before getting ready to leave. Just then, Jade appeared at the bathroom door.

"Mommy, what are you doing on the toilet? You KNOW I have to make before you!"

Uh-oh.

I'd already finished. I tried to be subtle as I flushed and pulled my pants back up.

"Ok, you go first."

"But you just went!" Jade said as her eyes began to tear up again.

"No-no, I didn't go really you go first."

So she sat down on the toilet.

"Hon, we're really, really late, are you sure you have to go?" I asked.

"Yes." And then, nothing.

I sat on the edge of the bathtub waiting. And waiting. And waiting.

Finally, she went.

"OK now vámonos!" I said as I began a hasty bathroom exit.

"No, now YOU have to go," Jade explained.

"Angel, I'm fine. I'll go later," I replied.

"You SAID you'd go AFTER me!" she exhaled. My girl has a mind like an elephant. It was time for the performance of a lifetime. I went through the motions.

"Can you please flush for me," I said.

"I didn't hear anything," she said. Evidently she also had the hearing of a hunting cat.

"You must not have been listening closely enough. Flush! Flush! We're really in a rush!" I sang.

She flushed. And finally, we left.

I rushed down our front stoop and motioned for Jade to follow. She stood on the top step and watched as a woman out walking her miniature Schnauzer came towards us. I grabbed Jade and hoisted her down to street level and put her down. My daughter attached herself to my hip, tugged on my jacket, and froze, scared of the dog.

As the dog-walking woman came upon us she said, "Don't worry, he's friendly."

"Well so is she," I responded. The dog-walking woman did a double-take and proceeded.

Generally, I'm against leashes for little kids, but at that moment I thought how much I wished I had one, maybe a retractable one, that I could tug on to get Jade moving forward!

I moved us swiftly down the street and on to school. Jade complained that I was moving too fast, but I reminded her if she wanted me to get home in time to go out for birthday dinner, that I had to actually make it to work.

The tone of my birthday had been set.

Forty-five minutes later, after dropping her at school and taking the subway, I entered the newsroom where I worked, hoping the news cycle that day would be manageable to cover. As the Executive Producer, and someone who's worked in the business long enough to know better, I shouldn't have even thought about it, lest I jinx myself.

First, we got word that the Federal Reserve was seizing control of insurance giant AIG, with an unprecedented $85 billion bailout in borrowed tax money.

Next, the Commerce Department reported new home construction had hit a 17-year-low.

Then stocks tumbled on fears that more large firms would potentially be in trouble. The Dow Jones Industrial Average lost 449 points by day's end.

Amid other news, there was a Constitution Day celebration we'd been requested to cover.

Oh, and there was that misprint in a telephone book that

had callers dialing a phone sex line while trying to reach a New Jersey political group, and then calling us to alert us as to what happened.

As I worked to make sure that we were on top of all of these stories and more, the day passed in a blur.

Before I knew it, it was 6 p.m., 6:30 p.m., 7 p.m. In a slapdash fashion, I anxiously logged out of my computer and headed home fielding phone calls and e-mails the entire time.

I arrived at 7:45 p.m., and lurched to open my apartment door.

"Mommy! Hurry! You're late! We have to go to the store before it closes!"

"The store?" I asked.

"The jewelry store!" Jade said and started jumping up and down. "And I want to pick out something after YOU pick out something," she added.

"Happy Birthday!" my husband exclaimed, as he marched us back out the door. "They close at 8 p.m., so let's go!"

I laughed, figuring we were heading to "Bejeweled," one of my daughter's favorite haunts, in which only the finest in rhinestones imported from China abound on hundreds, maybe even thousands of items.

But then my husband said, "Turn right." And he headed towards an artisan's jewelry store that I passed on the way to and from work, often stopping to admire the window displays.

"I wanted to let you pick out something special . . . some diamonds. After all, it's your 40th birthday," he said.

I looked at my watch. It was 7:52 p.m. The store was still open. We walked in, and the salesclerk said she was glad we'd made it. My husband had obviously called ahead.

I began peeking into the different cases, and it was as if all the earrings, bracelets, and necklaces were staring back at me each more beautiful than the next. I looked at my watch.

"What would you like to try on?" my husband asked.

"Maybe some diamond studs?" I said.

The saleswoman took out three pairs and began explaining the differences in the cuts and colors.

"Mommy, those are pretty! Can I get one for your birthday, too? Hurry and pick! Before the lady has to go home!"

I smiled and hugged my daughter. I kissed my husband. I thanked both of them for the kind gesture. I told the saleswoman I appreciated her help but said I'd have to come back another time when it wasn't so late. "Let's go get some dinner," I said.

"Are you sure?" my husband asked.

"Are you sure, Mommy?" Jade quizzed.

"Positive," I said smiling.

A girl should not have to pick out diamonds in a hurry. If the saying about diamonds being a girl's best friend were true, it follows that a girl certainly wouldn't want to rush to pick a best friend. Even if there was a small velvet box tied with a silk ribbon thrown in with the deal.

As we walked out of the store discussing where to go eat together, we meandered. We lollygagged. We strolled. Forty never felt so good.

the isle of needy, scary, screwed-up, misfit toys

By Liz Gumbinner ★ Mom 101

We don't all wear black in NYC you know. Some of us do wear a splash of charcoal after labor day.

I never entirely understood the Isle of Misfit Toys in that animated Rudolph movie. I mean the basic concept was clear: A train with square wheels, a fish who flew, a gay Charlie-in-the-Box doing a mean Charles Nelson Reilly impression. These were not "normal" toys. Thus, misfits. Got it.

(Of course there is the exception of the seemingly conventional doll who has inspired four decades of debate as to the possible reason for her misfit designation. My vote: Syphilis.)

In any case, I always hated their pariah status. To me, even at a young age, they seemed less like misfits than rejected playthings of spoiled kids with no imagination. Can you not play with an elephant with polka dots? Is a cowboy riding an ostrich less fun than a cowboy on a boring old horse? And what kind of parents would let their kids toss their toys for superficial flaws anyway? Didn't they teach them that what matters is not shallow surface traits like the shape of one's wheels but kindness, thoughtfulness, inner beauty?

Perhaps that's overstating my ten-year-old mindset. But I did feel bad for those toys. No toy should be without a child, as the miracle birth of Jesus Christ and MasterCard holiday commercials have taught us.

But now at last, I understand.

I get it.

There should be an Isle of Misfit Toys. Because there are some toys that don't deserve your love.

I first noticed it a few weeks ago when I was visiting my brother. He pointed out a little electronic keyboard toy of his daughter's that, get this, reminds you to play it. If you have stopped for a while, it admonishes, TIME TO PLAY THE PIANO.

Just like a mother calling "Time to wash up for dinner," or "Time to do your math homework," your child hears TIME TO PLAY THE PIANO. The voice is childlike and friendly, of course, but almost frighteningly upbeat. Not quite like a Stepford Wife; more like a preadolescent Tatum O'Neil after getting into her parent's cocaine stash. She's excited. She's eager. She doesn't realize how hard she's squeezing your arm as she pulls you into the second floor music room repeating, TIME TO PLAY THE PIANO.

Annoying, but all in all, relatively harmless.

Then I realized a a toy phone my daughter Thalia had received as a gift does essentially the same thing. She stops playing with it for a moment and it rings.

It calls you.

A toy that literally calls you, and tells you to play with it. Pick me up! Playyyyy with meeeeeee. I don't want to be aloooooone.

For a minute you might almost forget that it's just a plastic shell inhabited by a couple of AA batteries and not the ghost of Carol Anne.

(The call is coming from INSIDE THE HOUSE!)

I started to think, what is with all these needy toys? Toys that ask, no, demand that you play with them? My brother's keyboard toy doesn't ask you in that polite, sort-of British way, "Would you mind, I mean, if you're not really doing anything else . . . you know, just sort of (aw shucks) take a moment and play with me?" It implores you to play. Insists that you play. Or . . . or else. It's not normal.

And then came the drum.

Not any old drum, but one with electronic lights and bells and music and a switch with four different settings. With every flat-palmed smack of its taut plastic skin, it recites a letter of the alphabet, a number, a note of music. For all I know it can also predict the future and feng shui your apartment, this thing is that impressive.

At first Thalia amused herself with it, happy enough to strike the drum and hear the synthesized snare. But she's just a year old. After a brief spell the drum became less interesting than, say, the cat. Or a book. Or the petrified Cheerio that's been hiding under the couch for six weeks.

She tossed the drum aside.

That's when we heard the haunting chorus for the first time.

PLAY THE DRUM, EVERYONE PLAY THE DRUM.

And then again. PLAY THE DRUM EVERYONE, PLAY THE DRUM.

Finally, just one more eerie melodic warning before

knocking glasses off our shelves and mysteriously slamming our windows shut: PLAY THE DRUM EVERYONE, PLAY THE DRUM.

There are children in there, I tell you. Zombie children. Drum-playing freaky needy zombie children that want the world's toddlers to bend to their will. They will repeat this mantra over. And over. And over. Until you have no choice but to succumb to the percussive temptation. They do not want you to learn the alphabet or how to count to ten. They don't want you to eat or sleep, to kiss your mommy, or pet your dog. They just want you to hit that drum at any expense.

Children of the Drum.

And then after the third warning, like they never existed, the voices are gone.

And the house is quiet.

Too quiet if you ask me.

eau de colic

by **Vanessa Druckman** ★ **Chef Druck**

Bird just crashed in my window and smeared it with excrement. "Yum! Chocolate!" says Juliette. I better clean that up before she does.

It wasn't until Jack was born that I realized how easy I'd had it with just one child. I regretted every minute I had wasted whining about Bella's teething pains or her addiction to her unsightly pacifier. Instead of complaining, I should have been enjoying the good life, taking long afternoon naps and reading all the titles on Oprah's list, while my easy-going firstborn played quietly at my feet. But instead, my first few years of motherhood were spent stressing about cramming the maximum amount of IQ-building quality time into my days with my daughter.

Consequently, adjusting to life with two kids took some doing. After Jack was born, I basically didn't sleep for six months. I unsuccessfully tried every trick in the book to avoid our nightly date with colic: the car seat on top of the dryer, the swinging at high speed, and the driving exhausted through the dark neighborhood streets as our Subaru shook with screams. Only running in circles through the house clutching his rigid body in a tight football hold had any impact on the crying. And that only dulled his cries.

My two-year-old daughter just couldn't understand how her attentive, arts-and-crafts-loving mom had morphed into a weeping and screaming monster. She dealt with her confusion with guerrilla stealth attacks on the inconvenient crying lump I called her baby brother whenever my head was turned.

One sunny June morning, I decided to take some steps to regain control of my life by reintroducing some personal hygiene measures. Showering had become an optional luxury in my colic hell. I was starting to like the musky quality of my new personal fragrance, eau de colic, and my idea of dressing up had become putting on a fresh pair of sweatpants.

I installed Bella on my bed and turned on an Elmo Goes on the Potty video, enlisting my furry red monster-friend in the quest to have only one child in diapers, an unimaginable luxury. I left Jack crawling around on the floor (he couldn't actually move other than rotating in a circle) with a developmentally stimulating assortment of baby toys around him.

When I stepped into the shower, the steam was perfect, caressing me like an old lover. I wanted to close my eyes and stay in forever, but I didn't dawdle. I soaped, shampooed, and conditioned myself in less than five minutes. Although this was probably the quickest shower I had ever taken, when I emerged the world seemed a little brighter.

I didn't even take the time to fully wrap myself with a towel before checking on the kids. I opened the door and stood dripping water on the hardwood floor, staring at a deserted room. The door to the hallway was still closed, but the kids were nowhere to be seen. They had vanished. No Bella on the bed. No Jack on the floor. The only action was from Elmo bopping around on the TV screen. Guilt flooded me as I began hyperventilating and calling Bella's name.

A muffled voice answered me. "I'm here!" It seemed to be coming from behind the closet door. With a yank, I pulled it open and beheld the strangest sight: Bella, standing buck naked, next to Jack who was sitting up on top of a colorful pile of Steve's ties. His baby blue footie pajamas were soaking wet.

At first I felt relieved that a masked villain hadn't kidnapped my kids during my self-indulgent shower. But I just couldn't understand what had happened. Then, suddenly, the pieces of the puzzle fell into place. I knelt down and gave Jack a good sniff to confirm my hypothesis before beginning my interrogation.

"Bella, did you have an accident?"

"Yes mommy. But I cleaned it all up like a good girl!"

She was so proud of her resourcefulness, completely oblivious to how wrong it had been to use her baby brother as a human paper towel that I didn't have the heart to discipline her. Instead, I bid a silent good-bye to my shower paradise, put my personal hygiene on hold for a few more months, and began cleaning up the mess.

the photo shoot

by Melissa Chapman

Twitter is better than therapy—I get sympathy minus the hefty $150 price tag!

When I was six months pregnant with my now eight-year-old daughter, I was more than happy to trade in my pseudo Melanie Griffith working girl status minus the aqua-netted hair and sneakers for full-time stay at home motherhood. Instead of breathlessly running for subways and navigating the minefield of catty office politics, I had visions of waking up each morning to the sweet sounds of babies cooing, sunlight streaming through my windows, lounging in my pajamas, sipping coffee, while my little cherub sat snugly in her pink onesie staring up at me adoringly as I balanced a songbird on my finger like Julie Andrews.

Before I was inducted into AEY Me (also known as the sorority of the sleep deprived), where going to the bathroom with the door closed is strictly forbidden and talking on the phone with someone screaming in the background is mandatory, I'd envisioned motherhood to be the ultimate fairytale come true.

Of course any Similac-toting-mom with a diaper bag could've warned me that I was in for a rude awakening and those early years would be more akin to basic training in the army than a scene out of Mary Poppins. They probably should've clued me in that my days of sipping any liquid leisurely were officially over unless I could plan naptime during a Starbucks meet-up with a girlfriend and I probably wouldn't be afforded the luxury of sleeping past 6:30 a.m. on a weekend or weekday until my kids finally hit high school.

Suffice it to say, my writing career took a major back seat util by the grace of G-d, an editor at the *Staten Island Advance* took pity upon me, an out-of-work stay-at-home mom, and offered me the chance to write a weekly column. I guess she figured writing about life with kids, wouldn't be much of a stretch for me, considering I assured her I was a regular fixture on the mommy-and-me circuit and could change a dirty diaper with one-hand, while braiding hair with the other. To be perfectly honest ... I begged her for this extremely low-paying gig because I knew I needed an outlet to vent my feelings or I might just spontaneously combust. So having been guilt-tripped into giving me the job, she acquiesced and said she was going to send over a staff photographer to get my headshot taken for the column.

Unfortunately up until that point, my beauty regimen consisted of a two-minute rinse and repeat with my kids' strawberry-kiwi tear-free baby shampoo. I finally had a legitimate excuse to book a hair appointment! I'll never forget that first trip back to my prekid salon, it was like coming home again...aaah...the smell of peroxide and the roaring sound of blow-dryers. Heaven in a hair salon. It was almost too much for me to bear and I gladly forked over $300 for highlights.

The morning of my photo shoot, I was more than ready for my close-up; all I had to do was prep my then five-year-old daughter and one-and-a-half-year-old son for the photographer's visit. I tried in vain to explain to them in between commercial breaks from Noggin, how important it was that they behave on Mommy's very special day. That I was going to write all about what great children they were, and in return, all they had to do was get dressed in the outfits I had prepared for them, and put on their best-est, shiniest smiles. I figured it was simple enough and I even sweetened the pot with promises of chocolate and no bedtime. Of course my one and a half year old to his credit had no clue what I was talking about, and like all little siblings, took direct cues from his older sister who on that particular day, decided it was time to reveal she was indeed a bad seed who was hell-bent on destroying any good mother street-cred I might be trying to pull off with our community paper.

I spent the next 20 minutes pleading with her to get dressed because as time was running out, both my kids were running around stark naked. Jackson kept unfastening his diaper and Madison informed me that she wanted to have her picture taken in her birthday suit. I figured all bets were off. I was going to be exposed as a fraud—certainly unfit to write a column about the joys of parenting children. I envisioned the photographer stepping inside the perfect storm of chaos: a lunatic woman chasing after two naked kids, toys strewn all over the floor, with dishes piled high in the sink. Sure enough, just as the doorbell rang, I'd seconds earlier managed to wrangle my kids into a bumble bee costume and a Pocahontas ensemble.

As the photographer walked into the living room, I saw his cockeyed look of bewilderment at my kids in their get-ups. I then watched as he scanned my living room with a look of disgust, since the place now appeared as though it had been ransacked by an army of naked gypsy preschoolers. He then proceeded to ask me if I needed some time to straighten up. Of course, I had to restrain myself from punching out this obviously childless, couldn't be more than a 23-year-old, fresh out of college kid, who had no idea that just getting my kids to wear clothes was a feat in and of itself and that one day, when he became a parent, he too might find himself as I did just then with sweat dripping profusely from my brow (let's not even discuss my Secret-deprived armpits). I stifled the urge to deck him, smiled and said, "Sorry, this is as good as it gets." And my kids, while they managed to stand still long enough to get a few shots . . . refused to smile and could only muster expressions that looked more like deer caught in headlights, than the happy, well-adjusted kids I was banking my future columns on. I never found out what the photographer said when he went back to the newsroom that day—and even with over 100 columns under my belt, I'm still trying to find out if I'll ever be able to unlock all the secrets to AEY Me.

pressing rewind

by Andrea Forstadt

Having my world turned upside-down and thrown into a cyclonic tailspin was not on my radar that cold, cold January day.

The uber-organized woman that I pretend to be, I started my day with the typical list of To Do's. Make lunches for girls. Check. Pick up dry cleaning. Check. Get on those RSVPs whose deadlines passed a week ago. Maybe later. Although I'm no stranger to drama (Read: mom of two girls), having my world turned upside-down and thrown into a cyclonic tailspin was not on my radar that cold, cold January day.

The day sailed by like most until about 1 that afternoon when I had my first post-positive pregnancy test prenatal visit. Not to seem contrite but, having suffered a miscarriage the year before, the most I had hoped for was to still be pregnant. And with two pre-pubescent daughters in the mix, I wasn't even that married to the prospect. Following my miscarriage, my husband and I tried unsuccessfully to conceive for what seemed like an eternity and continuously extended our self-imposed deadlines by a month, then two, then six before pulling the plug. Ironically, my husband (or Mr. XY as I affectionately call him) was scheduled to have a vasectomy the very next day.

Looking back on that day, I was so pompously unphased and nonchalant around all of the obviously first time moms-to-be in the waiting room of my OB's office. So unsuspecting and glowing and open-minded combing through their mommy magazines while they waited. Me and my momitude silently shrugged and thought, "I could be teaching classes out here" before picking up *New York*. Looking back, I swear I can remember their "who's laughing now?" smirks as my trembling, pasty white shell of a body limped like a wounded soldier past them on my way out. In the 20 minutes since we last locked eyes, I had gone from feeling like rock star mom to the mother of all head-cases.

Pressing rewind.

Upon hearing my named called, I begrudgingly put down the article (I was hell-bent on finding out the end of the story on Sex Slaves and the City vs. the end of my story which I will soon learn has a much bigger, juicier (and by that I mean of the amniotic variety) twist. I walk into the exam room and spy the stirrups, happily anticipating getting horizontal for a much-needed respite from the breakneck pace of my day. Humbling, yet so, so worth it.

Enter Dr. Shock. We make a little small talk and begin my sonogram. I start to get excited and nervous, then more excited and more nervous as her silence spoke volumes.

One minute, then two... something had to be wrong. I can't stand it so I break the silence.

Me: "Is everything OK?"

Dr. Shock: "I need to concentrate, give me a minute."

Another minute, then two.

Me: "Can you please tell me something? Anything? Am I even still pregnant?"

Dr. Shock: "Let me turn on the overhead flat screen so you can see what's going on."

Shit.

Dr. Shock: OK. See this? (Pointing to an empty bubble-shaped blob.) This is baby A.

Me: Baby A? Great thanks. I've really got to go. Need to make it home before the school bus. See you in a month?

Dr. Shock: And this, I believe, is Baby B.

Me: No, that's just a smudge on the screen. Your cleaning crew must have missed a spot. Grounds for dismissal. Anyway, like I said, gotta go.

Dr. Shock: No, I'm pretty sure that's...

Me: No. No, no, no, no, no. no. It can't be. Get that Baby B off of the screen. Back to you, Baby A!

Dr. Shock: Chuckle, chuckle, chuckle.

Me: Seriously. Seriously?

Dr. Shock: Andrea, a woman's chances for conceiving multiples increases significantly after 35.

Me: Guess I missed that memo.

So, there I was, staggering out of the office, down the elevator, out to the parking lot. Watching the entire scene from up above, my first encounter with an out-of-body experience. I fall into my car and fumble for my cell, trying to compose my thoughts before I call my poor, unsuspecting husband.

Seeing my name come up on his caller ID he joyfully answers the phone. "Hi honey." Sobs pre-empted words. He winced before guessing that I had another miscarriage. "Worse," I replied. The only logical "worse" was unspeakable, so my husband, sounding instantly terrified, asked if they had found "something" (read: tumor). Now, I'm honestly not sure if I really believed this to be true or I was just trying to soften the ultimate blow, but again, I replied, "Worse than even that." He pleaded, "What could be worse than that?" So I spilled the news in a strange half laugh, half cry and in an instant, amidst all of this raw emotion, fell madly in love with my husband again with his sigh of relief, sense of humor, and typical guy affirmation of "Damn my boys really can swim."

Of course, by the time he came home from work that night he was singing a slightly different tune as I stared at my sonogram pictures in disbelief and found therapy in a half-gallon of Edy's and a Jon & Kate Plus Eight marathon. I went to bed not quite embracing my new reality yet with the amazing realization that this is exactly what I wanted. One lesson for me: Be careful what you wish for, 'cause you just might get it all (thank you, Daughtry); one lesson for my husband: This pool is officially closed!

the harried mom
and her half-trained twins

by Cheryl Lage ★ Twinfatuation ★
Author of Twinspiration

Keeping it honest with Daddy who's coming home late: The trash-can-filling Happy Meal boxes aren't hidden under the Kroger flyer...

After becoming a parent, casual conversation with strangers at the mall tends to cross over into a far more personal realm. As a mother of twins, it's no holds barred. Case in point: my kids and I were sitting at the food court savoring our Chic-Fil-A nuggets when a somewhat frenzied-looking young mom approached us, "Excuse me," she said. "But I need to know: Is your daughter still in diapers?"

Judging from her thinly-veiled expression of panic, I could tell this wasn't just a curious inquiry from a mother wondering when to start potty-training her child, but rather the heated panic of a woman whose stroller-bound daughter wore the gleeful expression of one joyfully—precariously—going au naturale after sullying the last diaper in the bag.

"Sorry," I said, "Mine wear undies now, but I'm sure if you head over to mall's playground area, just around the escalator, you'll find some other moms who might have an extra diaper to lend you."

I then returned my attention to my toddler twosome, a proud smile on my lips, "Didn't that make you feel good to know you don't need diapers anymore?"

"Yes, Mommy," chirped my son, providing the answer he clearly knew was expected.

The waffle fries had my daughter's attention as she emitted a half-hearted, "Mmm-hmm."

That night, as we tucked everyone in and said our prayers, we (mostly me) voiced our thankfulness for all we've learned (namely, how to use the potty) and the example we can set for other kids preparing to tread the same path.

Dare I speak too soon?

Three a.m.

"M-o-o-o-o-o-o-m-m-m-m-m-m-m-m-m-y!"

Upon entering the lava-lamp lit nursery, I could see Sarah standing in the very corner of her tented crib. Training panties, Tinkerbell nightgown, sheet, and fleecy blanket all drenched in a daughter-described (and dramatically minimized), "Little accident."

Knowing she's in the latter stages of the potty-training process, these late-night, deep-sleep accidents are not totally unexpected. Groggily, I stripped the bed and restocked it with sleep-inducing supplies, all the while making a mental note to purchase a new vinyl protective cover the next day, as hers had a mattress jeopardizing rip.

Babies-R-Us (the only location in town that stocks vinyl crib mattress covers) continues to be an entertaining destination, despite the fact our twosome can hardly be considered "babies" anymore. Of course the 50-cent Big Bird jet plane ride at the store's entrance serves as a great motivator for appropriate in-store behavior.

We hadn't been shopping ten minutes when Darren erupted with an urgent, "POTTY, MOMMY!!!"

Navigating the double stroller toward the family bathroom with the adrenaline-charged speed of an Olympian luge-launcher, I raced against the biology of boy parts. I lost.

Stroller seat? Saturated.

Pants? Puddled.

Mom's patience? Over-taxed.

Wedging the stroller so that it kept the stall door ajar, allowing me arms-length access and sightline to the strapped-in and highly-amused Sarah, off came Darren's shoes, socks, pants and wringable Thomas the Tank Engine undies.

Wisely, I continue to carry dry clothes for instances such as these.

Woefully, I neglected to pack a plastic bag in which to place any urine-dripping duds.

Into our thermal waterproof lunchbag they went. Delicious.

Twenty-four hours had yet to elapse since my pride-inflated declaration of the diaper's demise in our twin-blessed household.

Alas, our journey to plural potty prowess continues . . .

Moral of the story? If you see the three of us chomping on chicken nuggets at the food court, please . . . no personal questions. Just ask us how to get to the mall playground.

the letter

by Sherry Shealy Martschink ★ Ex Marks the Spot

Today is National Visit Your Relatives Day. If you're kin to me, please ignore.

I've been harried longer than most of today's moms have been alive! We're talking decades here.

Way back yonder (for you non-Southerners, "yonder" can refer to time, space, distance, and just about anything else when convenient!) I was a state senator and mother of three awkward-aged children when I became a candidate for lieutenant governor.

Yep, I was running alright. And harried.

There were Senate duties, campaign duties, end-of-school year activities, recitals, sports programs, and more.

THE LETTER

Not long after I was elected to the South Carolina state senate, I was in Columbia, our state capitol, for work. I called home.

When my oldest child answered the phone, she sounded a bit distant, like something was wrong. After a bit of conversation, I asked her if something was bothering her.

First she said there wasn't anything wrong. Then she admitted, yes, there was a problem. A letter for me had arrived in the mail.

Well, that didn't sound like a problem to me. After all, letters arrive every day.

Before I reveal what disturbed her, let me tell you that the three children were so happy their mom had won the hard-fought election. In fact, they were ecstatic. No, they didn't really know what the Senate was or what it all involved. They just knew "we," all of us, had won.

Winning the election was just the beginning of a lifetime of chaos, turmoil, excitement, and unknowns for the whole family.

On this particular day, though, my daughter had gotten the mail after school. As we talked on the phone, she was scared to tell me what had arrived in the mail.

Finally, though, she told me. She was tearful and her voice trembled as she said into the phone: "Mom, a letter came today addressed to 'The Horrible Sherry Martschink.'"

OK, I confess. This was politics. Lots of people called me lots of names. Most didn't put name-calling on the envelopes, though.

This was not one of those times of name-calling, however. Actually, the envelope was addressed to "The Honorable Sherry Martschink" instead of "The Horrible Sherry Martschink." My daughter had misread the envelope, and she was scared to tell me about this mail!

On another occasion, it was late in the afternoon and I was driving the 100+ miles from the state capitol to home when my daughter called and said, "Oh, mom, I forgot to tell you that the dinner and program for the band and band parents is tonight at 7. And I volunteered you to bring dessert. I told them you'd bring some of your chocolate-chip cookies."

It was about 5:45 then and I was still an hour away!

The crazy thing is that this was not unusual. My children must have been the only ones in the world who decided to let mom know at the last minute, OK, perhaps at the last hour about school programs and extracurricular events. (On one occasion, it was late at night when my daughter told me she had to have a lamb's costume the next day!! And I don't sew at all.)

I wanted to attend each and every event in which my children were involved but couldn't make 100% of the activities. I made an effort to get to most, especially the ones my son said he'd rather me not attend.

By the way, it was that kind of request by my son that made me think I should attend PTA meetings under an assumed name.

On one particular night, I was scheduled as the after-dinner speaker for an organization, and this time, fortunately, it wasn't far from home. I was running for lieutenant governor. It was important to meet as many people as possible, to shake as many hands as possible, and to get as many commitments as possible.

We were almost through with the meal, when I got an urgent message to call home. I excused myself from the head table to go make that call.

I quickly learned that one of my daughters (Tiffany) was on the way to the emergency room; she had a toothpick stuck in her thigh! Yes, a toothpick stuck in her thigh.

As I headed back into the meeting room, I wondered how this explanation would sound to the group. Well, it didn't really matter because it was the truth, no matter how far-fetched it sounded. So, I apologized to the group and said I had to go to the hospital to meet my daughter who had a toothpick stuck in her thigh.

As it turned out, there had been a toothpick hidden down in the carpet. The children had been playing when that toothpick and her outer thigh somehow "met." She couldn't get the toothpick out; a neighbor tried and couldn't get it out either. He said it appeared the muscle had tightened around the toothpick, making it impossible to remove easily.

The doctor deadened the area and did whatever was necessary to relax the muscle, then removed the toothpick. There was no permanent damage. Thank goodness.

This had to be one of strangest "emergencies" known to motherhood, I thought. I was wrong. Later that night, one of the women who had been at the meeting called to check on my daughter. We were talking about the strange story when she said she totally understood. When her daughters were young, she got a call at work one day to come home because a daughter had gotten Barbie's clothes stuck up her nose.

I don't know if I ever heard the explanation on that one. Quite frankly, I'm not certain I want to know how that child got Barbie's clothing stuck in her nose.

Ah, the joys of motherhood!

if it looks like a duck

by Beth Feldman ★ Role Mommy

I'm changing my middle name to Procrastination.

While my daughter was at school yesterday, I was given a very important assignment—purchase a Webkinz duck for her friend who was having a birthday slumber party that night. My daughter was so concerned I would get her request wrong that she actually drew me a picture of the duck and slipped it into my pocket.

After dropping her off at school, I worked all day and by the time I turned around, about five hours had passed and I hadn't yet picked up the present. And so, for a few fleeting moments, I stepped away from my keyboard, hopped in my car, and drove to the closest place I could find that I thought carried the brand spankin' new Webkinz duck.

I arrived at a trendy store in my neighborhood populated by the snottiest teenagers I've ever met. Since the boutique normally sells overpriced jeans, T-shirts, outerwear, and dresses for kids and teens, they had no use for little old me who was searching in the back of the store for a Webkinz duck. As I dug through the pile of stuffed animals, I found what I thought was the duck my daughter had asked for. I proudly walked it up to the register and when one of the girls told me they were on sale and were charging $20 for two Webkinz, I thought I had found the bargain of the century and picked up a unicorn to add to my perfect birthday gift.

As I was checking out, I decided to make a little small talk with the pretentious teens behind the register.

"I'm so glad I didn't have to drive all over town for that duck Webkinz," I blurted.

"Oh, you mean the platypus?" commented one of the girls, whose hair was hanging over one eye. I believe that was some kind of new hair style, but to me, it just looked weird and messy.

"Platypus? You mean there are other ducks?" I responded, having a sinking feeling in my stomach that I bought the wrong Webkinz.

"Oh I don't know if there are other ducks, we just have this one," the teen responded, as she handed me a cellophane bag with my tissue paper wrapped Webkinz tucked inside.

When I returned to the school to pick up my daughter, she immediately asked me the telltale question.

"Did you get the duck?"

"Sure I got the duck, it's in the house."

"Well what does it look like? Does it have chubby cheeks?"

"It kind of has a long neck."

"Mommy!!!! That's not the duck. That's Google, the Platypus!!! We need to get the duck. Where did you get that Webkinz?"

I told her the name of the store and she knew in an instant where I had gone wrong.

"Mommy, that store only sells old Webkinz. The platypus is from last year!"

Mystery solved. The reason that overpriced store was selling Webkinz at a cheaper price was because all they had were the outdated stuffed animals that no kid who is plugged into the Webkinz craze would purchase in a million years. What a rip-off.

So what did we do after my daughter realized I had inadvertently purchased the wrong duck? We hopped in the car of course and zipped off to the neighborhood toy store, arriving minutes before they closed.

As my daughter ran inside and scanned the shelves, she instantly found it.

"The last duck!!! We found the last duck!!!"

After asking the man at the cash register for what seemed like the Hope Diamond, he handed it over, and my daughter shared the story of her mother's duck blunder.

"I'm so glad you have the duck. My mom bought the wrong one and I knew that you had the duck and that's what my friend wanted for her birthday. I can't believe we got the last duck!"

With our crisis averted, we took our duck, went on our merry way and headed off to the slumber party and the moment we arrived, my daughter's friend took the package out of her hands, ripped off the paper and was thrilled to receive her duck. Don't kids wait until after cake to open presents anymore? With that, I knew I had made my daughter's night because she had selected the right gift and I went home to figure out what I was going to do with Google the Platypus.

Moral of the story ... just because it looks like a duck, it doesn't necessarily mean it's the right duck.

night of horror,
i.e. the night the wireless went out

by Beth Blecherman ★ SVMoms Blog & Tech Mama

Hit official mom wall of exhaustion— Delegated kids to neighbors, closed door & have not left my bed all afternoon. Only have energy 2 Twitter.

I had just purchased some chicken with the good intention of putting together a nice home-cooked meal for my husband and three boys. This would be a welcome and healthy deviation from the pattern of takeout and frozen food that had been my mainstay for the previous few weeks due to a heavy work schedule. Blogging day and night, managing my personal blog, Twitter feed and Facebook updates, as well as fulfilling my "Chief Technology Mom" role for my national network of Mom blogs had left me a bit short in the "Culinary Mom" department at home. I was determined to spend more time in the kitchen.

It was 4 p.m., an hour or two earlier than my usual "oh nuts, it's dinner time and I've been working all day . . . what's frozen or not moldy that can be microwaved and served for dinner" rush. And then it happened. With no notice, the power went out in our house. I later found out that on this beautiful, windy spring day, some trees had fallen somewhere in Northern California causing the one thing in Silicon Valley that is considered a real emergency: a power outage.

In their recorded customer-service message, Pacific Gas & Electric estimated that power would be restored by 9 p.m. OK. Time for some decisions before the sun went down and three boys began to re-enact X-Men super hero battles as hunger tested their stomachs, common sense, and true gentlemen-like nature. I called my husband, who promised to buy ice on the way home from work in order to keep the chicken from spoiling in a slowly warming refrigerator. I could tell he was happy, anticipating thinking of a blog-free, candlelit evening, and conversation with his wife. He would HEAR about my day rather than reading about family adventures in my Twitter feed and blog posts.

What about dinner? My first thought was to break out the earthquake emergency kit of water, power bars, candles, and duct tape (why is tape in the earthquake kit anyway?) and I was relieved. No requirement to cook dinner when the stove doesn't work, right? Time for takeout, which always puts me in a Happy Mommy mood. But my happy mood changed quickly when I realized that the true challenge was NOT nourishment, it was living without an Internet connection for one night. And that sent shivers down my spine.

I started hyperventilating. No Internet access meant that I could not finish the important website coding I had scheduled for after the kids went to sleep. It also meant no blogging, e-mailing, Twittering, Facebooking, or other online social networking that is my evening social lifeblood as well as profession. Making matters worse, we had updated all of our home phones to wireless as well, so no power also meant no regular phone service. Our "old fashioned" corded phones, so handy when the power went out, had been confiscated by my boys for use as "Bat-phones" and were nowhere to be found. I was completely cut off.

Well, I thought, at least I can use my Smartphone for phone and Internet access until the power comes on.

I checked the battery on my Smartphone and to my horror discovered that several long conference calls that day had greatly reduced the battery charge. NOOOOoooooooooo! What's a Techie Mom to do?

Think quickly...the boys had to be fed and I had to find a way to charge my Smartphone. Get food and charge phone. Hmmmmm . . . think quickly. Eureka! The CAR! I realized that driving to get takeout not only would solve the problem of what to serve my kids for dinner, but also would charge up my phone while I was driving. I packed the boys, now armed with flashlights for their personal episode of "Justice League on Planet Darkness," into the car and we aimed our spaceship named "Minivan" toward the Sushi Universe one light year away.

I stretched out the drive as much as I could, trying to get at least three bars of battery on the phone while watching the sun start to set. We needed to get home before dark to take quick showers, find more flashlights and light candles. Pulling into my driveway, I felt accomplished. My Smartphone battery was partly charged and dinner was ready to be served. Before I got out of the car, I Twittered from my Smartphone for what I thought was one last time that night. "I'm home, no power, cellphone battery is low." It was a desperate message to the outside world, similar to what I imagined Tom Hanks would have done in *Cast Away* if only that movie had been made just a few years later. Several minutes passed and I melodramatically updated my Twitter community that they may not be hearing from me for a while, but that "my boys and I are warm and safe." As if my Twitter followers could not get by without my Tweets that night.

My husband came home to a dark, candlelit house and was thrilled, in a neighborhood without power, to see takeout Japanese food on the kitchen table. We put the kids to bed after their Jedi light saber pajama battle, flashlights by their sides, and sat down to a late dinner of Udon soup. As he asked me about my day, the power was suddenly restored.

We were connected to the outside world again! Yes! But could we leave the computer off until after dinner?

the secret

by Meredith Jacobs ★ Modern Jewish Mom

Having really good hair day. Must renew driver's license A.S.A.P.

I stopped weighing myself when the scale read 198 (notice I didn't write "when I weighed 198," I wrote "when the scale read 198" as if this was an issue that purely described the state of the scale). True, I gave birth soon after and true, I lost all the weight (plus an additional ten pounds!) without really working on it, so maybe this was just how my body reacted to pregnancy. This was now my second pregnancy and I was gaining weight at the same rate as my first when I was on bed rest and thought I could blame the pounds on inactivity. Obviously, I was wrong, as chasing after an 18 month old did not prevent me from packing on ten pounds in between each and every OB appointment. At one point, my doctor asked me if I was eating a lot of fruit. Thinking he was worried about my nutrition, I answered him honestly that no, I really don't like fruit, but I was eating a lot of vegetables. He said that he wasn't worried about the fruit he was just trying to figure out where all the weight was coming from. "Oh!" I said, "it's the cookies!" (I enjoyed my pregnancies.)

But the thing is, no one really told me I was huge. (And I mean HUGE.) They told me I was "adorable." And, in my cute, cute, cute swingy (roomy) maternity tops that my mom had bought for me in a schmaltzy pregnancy boutique in Philadelphia, how was I to think otherwise? I happily waddled around my second pregnancy with toddler in tow.

And when my protruding stomach wiped out an entire tabletop display at the interior decorator's, I was the only one in the store to look surprised.

Pregnancy does things to a mom's mind. Tiny changes occur in our otherwise capable brains that, like the weight gain, we fail to notice or, even if we kind of notice, fail to recognize the true power of the change. And I was in full denial that pregnancy was my kryptonite and that my Supermom status had been compromised.

By the way, I was/am "Supermom." The really, truly annoying, "Martha" kind of Supermom. I lived off the buzz of self-congratulatory pride I fed myself knowing that I was better than all the other moms who hired baby sitters or (gasp) nannies. I saw them in the various music/ballet/gym/art/drama/story-time classes that overwhelmed my schedule. Those non-moms who gave real moms a break. Ha! I didn't need them! Who cared that Sofie was up all night and woke at 5 a.m.? Who cared that my pregnancy restricted me from the life-saving caffeine? When Sofie said "doggy," we wrote the word "DOG" on her easel in the family room and then drew a picture of a dog and then went on a walk to find a dog and then went to the library to get out books about dogs. We built cars and puppet theaters out of refrigerator boxes. We went to museums and puppet shows and musical performances. When YoYo Ma came on the radio, I identified him to Sofie and explained to her that he is a famous cellist (and then we went to the library to find pictures of cellos and went to Barnes & Noble to buy YoYo Ma CDs to listen to). I shopped at the organic market and made her every meal. Only I, Supermom, could do that for my child. I was AWESOME!!!

So I couldn't tell anyone when I locked her in the car.

I'm admitting it now. Now, for the world to see and only now because it may help another, younger Supermom know that it's OK to not be perfect (and, now that Sofie is about to become a Bat Mitzvah and is an amazing, talented, incredible kid who obviously wasn't traumatized at all by the incident, I can feel safe to laugh about it).

But I behaved in a most unsupermom like way. To continue the superman reference, I became "Bizarro Supermom."

Driving around with Sofie, armed with information gleaned from watching Oprah's interview with Gavin De Becker and having actually purchased (but not read) his book *Protecting the Gift* I was in the habit of making sure we were all safely locked in our big, candy red ('cause it's "sporty") minivan. I would load Sofie into her car seat, lock and shut her door before walking around to the driver's side, where I would unlock just my door, get in, and lock the door before I closed it. At no point were either Sofie or I in the car with any door unlocked and thus available for some crazed carjacker to jump in and hurt or abduct us (some may call it overboard, I prefer "Supermom").

So, there we were, first thing in the morning, (I, hugely pregnant and sufficiently sleep deprived), nestled into the parking space in front of the supermarket. Another day of errands had begun. I sighed, turned off the ignition, opened the door while depressing the button to lock it as soon as the door pulled open, heaved my body out of the car, shut the door and walked around the minivan to Sofie's door at which point I realized my keys were still in the ignition.

Did I mention it was hot outside?

Did I mention that 11 years ago I didn't have a cell phone?

I freaked out a little (I didn't want to scare Sofie, who was not yet concerned about why I hadn't taken her out of her car seat).

Oh, did I mention she HATED being in her car seat and would cry when the car stopped?

Fun.

What would I do? I couldn't run into the shopping center because that would mean I was abandoning Sofie! I started yelling "Help! Help! I've locked my baby in the car!" In between SOS (or SMB) calls, I would squeeze my face as far as it would go into the window vents in the back of the van (you know, those small, narrow windows in the way, way back that open out and purely help with air circulation—thank goodness I always left those open). Anyway, I pressed my face into them and sang "ABCDEFG, HIJK, LMNO, P..." (the ABCs always soothed Sofie). Meanwhile, Sofie was kinda looking around like "What? Number one, where the hell is Mommy? And, number two, why do I hear Mommy singing?") At which point, I would worry that she was worried because she couldn't see me, so I would run back to her window and smile and make silly faces and then run back to the vent and sing and then pause and yell for help.

Did I mention I was hugely pregnant?

Finally, a woman walked through the parking lot with a cell phone, called the local police, who came in five minutes, pulled apart the window sealant, unlocked the door and released Sofie. All in all, I would say it was a ten-minute ordeal. But it felt like hours.

I was rattled.

Sofie was fine.

Later that night, when Jonathan came home and asked about our day, I rattled off all the unremarkable incidents. Sofie piped up, "Mommy locked me in da car."

"What, honey?" asked Jonathan.

"Right, sweetie, we saw a flag today," I interrupted.

"No! Locked in da car!"

"Yes, it was a big flag." (It did somehow sound like she was talking about a flag. This was truly awful of me because Sofie had a terrible articulation problem and needed me to interpret for her. Of course I knew what she was saying, but Jonathan didn't, and I wasn't about to let her rat me out. Daughter or not, I had a rep to protect! I had become Bizarro Supermom.)

Years and years passed and we never spoke about it. Sofie has forgotten but I never did. Just the other week, Jonathan and I were sitting on the couch watching television.

"I don't want there to be any secrets between us. I need to tell you something."

Jonathan braced himself.

"When Sofie was a baby and I was pregnant with Jules, I accidentally locked her in the car."

"So, what happened?"

"A woman walked by with a cell phone, we called the police and they came and let her out."

"Okay. Why didn't you tell me at the time?"

"I don't know. Pregnancy brain disorder?"

"Do you have any other secrets?"

"Nope."

"Can we finish watching the show?"

busted

By April Welch, CPO ★ Simply Organized Online

[TEXT TO HUSBAND]
Have begun drinking. It was either that or kill the teenager. Be sure to drive safely. See you when you get home.

Being the only girl in a household has its pros and cons.

Pros:

Life in the spring (fishing season) and fall (hunting season) becomes a guaranteed quiet time of the year. Allowing peaceful moments of solitude and plenty of time to do whatever I want

Once a month I'm left completely alone when I gather up M&M's, cheddar popcorn, and a bottle of wine. As my supplies begin to surface, the boys (including the one I'm married to) head for the opposite end of the house, where all things testosterone reside, while I head to my bedroom with a movie and some Midol

Cons:

Trying to understand how it feels to go through Sex Ed in the fifth grade as a boy (this was an entirely alien experience and not one I want to repeat any time soon!).

I'm often out-voted on things like being muddy, X-Box games, and guns (Nerf and air soft).

One such thing I was out-voted on years ago: allowing the kids to watch the TV show Cops. It has now become a Saturday night staple in our family time.

My Fireman husband reasoned, this reality show, provided the true version of what it was like to make poor choices in our society and that, as boys, our kids should understand what could be waiting for them at the other end of being a less than stellar community member. What can I say? He made sense.

Although, when my youngest son was seven years old he had brought the show to life every time we passed someone who had been pulled over. As soon as he saw flashing lights he would yell (very loudly) "BUSTED" with an unbelievable emphasis on the B. When friends were around I would smile politely and respond with: "Look at that, we have our own modern day deputy!," but in private I would explain to him that it was rude to embarrass the poor soul who was clocked doing 80 in a 30 m.p.h zone.

Of course, my husband found this extremely entertaining. About the time this family night tradition began, we relocated ourselves to Small Town USA, approximately two hours (and a mountain pass) away from the fire department that employs my husband. Not to worry though, he has that crazy 24 hour schedule. (Allowing me peace and solitude at least every 8 days.) I used this opportunity to start my own business as a professional organizer (helping folks clear clutter from their lives). With a houseful of boys, I've got plenty of practice!

Fast forward to after we've broken this "BUSTED" habit. Circumstances arose that I needed to drive my husband's commuter car home from Grandma's house with the kids. (Leaving Dad at work.) No problem, right?

Hmmm. Wrong!

There's a spot coming down the pass where the speed limit decreases by 10 m.p.h. and YES, there was a speed trap set up that day. Lucky me!

I no sooner see the sign, a cop comes racing toward me in the opposing lane (lights blaring) and my youngest (in his most reserved manor) states "Someone's Busted!"

I was thinking about how proud I was of him until the officer and I were near enough to see one another. Then, I realized he was pointing at ME to pull over! (Quite angrily I should add too!) All of the sudden I have another cop behind me with lights flashing (I must have appeared armed and dangerous with my two young accomplices in the back seat!) So, I begin to slow down and pull off to the side.

The moment my son realized I was the one who was "busted" his eyes became as large as saucers! I calmly told him it was all right and not to worry.

When the cop approached he requested the regular documentation "License, insurance and registration. Please."

"Sure, here's my license. This is my husband's commuter car so I'm not sure where he keeps the . . ."

I had opened the glove box to expose a completely STUFFED area. Even if I had an hour I'm not sure I would have found what I was looking for! I begin digging through receipts, napkins, manuals and miscellaneous papers thinking the whole time that he had a little Car Organizing 101 coming his way!

In the meantime, my youngest was sitting in the back

seat torn between the awe of seeing a police officer so close up (with guns and everything!) and the sheer terror that the next thing to happen would be his Mom thrown to the ground, pummeled by every officer available, tasered, handcuffed, and stuffed in the back of the squad car!

Back to the driver's seat . . . Apparently, I'm no different than my peers when it comes to providing unnecessary personal information in nervous situations (that is, if I'm comparing myself to the suspects on the show). While I fumbled through the glove box I mention that I'm a Professional Organizer and you would think the important documents would be "right here on top"! "Even many of my clients have been able to successfully organize their important pulled-over documents!" (Yes, I really do think that came out of my mouth!)

I then apologized that things weren't more readily available. He grunted or chuckled, I'm still not sure since I never looked up to distinguish if I had irritated him more or if he found me completely amusing!

I was finally able to produce an expired insurance card and an old registration. He accepted this and headed back to check it out.

Time for damage control. I'm fully aware of the fear swirling around in my poor child's imagination and do my best to assure him the worst that could happen would be a speeding ticket. (No silver bracelets for Mommy today).

I still don't know if it was seeing my son's shocked face or the guy feeling sorry for this poor woman who teaches everyone else how to be organized and obviously doesn't rub off on her own husband, but he let me go with just a warning.

Phew!

As soon as we made it home the kids tumbled out of the car and went running inside —this is routine (everyone's headed for a bathroom). As I started my mad dash, I hear my youngest state: "Dad! Mom got BUSTED!" Instead of heading for the restroom, he went straight for the phone to call his dad!

In the weeks that followed, all anyone heard about was how I was BUSTED and lived to tell about it!

a trip to remember

By Jeanne Muchnick

My adorable, angelic-faced toddler has turned into an eyeliner-laden monosyllabic 16-year-old.

Where oh where has my little girl gone?

The adorable, angelic-faced toddler who used to say, "Your hair looks pretty today Mommy," "Sit next to me, Mommy," and "I wish you could stay home with me and not go to work today," has turned into an eyeliner-laden monosyllabic 16 year old who only talks to me when she wants a ride to her friend's house or needs me to find her black leggings that she swore she put in the laundry but are no doubt growing stiff with dirt from lying on her bedroom floor for weeks.

It wasn't always this way. We used to hug. We used to color. We used to spend hours at the mall together grabbing burgers and fries between scouring through sales racks at Nordstrom's. But somewhere around the 15-year mark, she started to distance herself from me, get new bffs who I hardly know, started lining her hazel eyes with kohl-colored liner, and walked around the house glued to her iPod, computer, and phone (often all at the same time).

Which is why, when a long weekend business trip to San Diego came up, I figured I'd ask her to join me. It would be a great way for us to bond. The conference had promised excursions for guests while allowing me time for business. But no sooner had I asked her and she'd agreed that our usual bickering took over.

"Have you packed?"

"I WILL Mom."

"OK. Don't forget."

"I WON'T Mom."

"Especially remember your toothbrush."

"I heard you the first time."

"OK, because it's always twice the price in the gift shop if you have to buy a new one."

"What's the big deal? I have my own money."

"I know, but it's a waste."

"But if it's MY money, why do you care?"

"Because I do."

And then, "Why do you keep interrogating me? It's just a toothbrush!"

"I know but..."

"ARGH! Will you stop talking to me?" And then: door slam.

Day of departure. I have my bag at the front door waiting for my husband to take us to the airport. Corey's clothes are still all over the floor. She's barely awake. God forbid she could have cancelled her plans last night and come home at a decent hour to pack. Now she's rushing, no doubt stuffing dirty clothes into her carry-on.

"Do you have everything?" I call from downstairs where my heart is palpitating (I like to leave extra time when traveling). "We need to get going."

"I KNOW, Mom!" she yells back.

"Just make sure you have your toothbrush." I say.

"Mom, I KNOW how to pack."

Hubby gives me the warning look. I back off. "I just hope she knows I'm not wasting my money on stuff if she forgot it," I say to him.

"She knows," he says.

Fast forward to our lovely five-star room overlooking the ocean. The sunshine. The duvet covers. The balcony that overlooks the ocean. The peaceful mother/daughter détente. "This is nice!" Corey says. "I love it here."

"I'm glad," I say.

We inspect our room together, kvelling over the up-to-the-minute hairdryer in the room, the decadent rosemary smelling shampoos, the complimentary nuts and waters, the flat-screen TV, the view.

I go off to my meeting, leaving Corey happy at the pool (with sunscreen I packed of course). We meet for dinner. She has a nice glow from the sun. I have a nice glow from the wine that comes with our meal. We talk. Her battery died on her cell phone so she can't text her friends. The end result: She actually tells me about school and how her English teacher just got engaged and about a new project she's working on with the student council. She asks me about my writing and how my meeting went. She's the sweet girl I used to know, inquisitive and curious and caring about my opinion. I think I'm so smart planning this trip together. We walk on the beach before hitting our hotel room and go to sleep to the sounds of the lapping waves outside.

It's not until the morning when I'm rushing to another meeting and Corey is getting ready for an excursion to the zoo that I hear a faint "Uh-oh" from behind the bathroom door. "What?" I yell over the din of *The Today Show*.

"I didn't pack any underwear."

"You're kidding." I say.

"Nope," she calls out. "Think they'll have any at the gift shop?"

"No, I don't," I answer sternly. "That's not something they carry." (Considering she wears Victoria Secret thongs.)

"What am I going to do?" she comes out with a towel wrapped around her. "Should I wear what I already have?"

"Absolutely not," I say, "Though we can rinse it out later. For now, you can wear mine. I always pack extras."

"Ugh, that's gross," she says.

"They're not gross," I counter, "They're clean. Here." I handed her the underwear. They look ginormous, even to me, but I've always been one of those Jockey girls from the 70s who still likes a covered up look.

"You've GOT to be kidding," she says. "No way."

"It's either that or go au natural," I suggest. "We're only here for a long weekend and I'm not running out to buy you new underwear."

"I'd rather wear my bathing suit," she says.

"Then wear that. But you can't wear that all weekend," I say. "It'll get skanky."

"Yes I can," she counters.

"Fine," I give in. "Do whatever you want," I say as I pick up my briefcase.

"Nice attitude," she says.

"I'm just trying to help."

"Well it's a stupid suggestion."

"Well it was stupid of you to pack the day we were leaving. I KNEW you'd forget something"

"Well I was busy. And you're the mom. You're supposed to have reminded me."

"I DID remind you."

"No you didn't. You only reminded me about my toothbrush. Which I brought... so hah!"

"You're impossible," I say

"No, you're impossible," she says.

Door slam (me walking out of the hotel room).

Fast forward to the afternoon when we're supposed to meet up. I'm walking back to the room when I figure, what the hell? I'll stop at the hotel gift shop to see if they carry anything remotely resembling Victoria's Secret panties, when I bump into Corey. "Did you ask the sales lady?" I say when I see her. "Nope," she says, "I just got here." "Ask me what?" the librarian-looking sales lady asks after overhearing us. "Oh, we're looking for underwear," I say. After all, the lady looks like my mother all sweet and nice and what harm is there in asking? Corey shoots me a darting look that dares me to go the next step. Her mouth puckers up like she's about to blow her top and I realize, despite the fact that we're the only ones in the store, that I've gone too far by merely mentioning the word "underwear."

"Oh we were looking for something kitschy," I say, trying to recover/somehow make it all less embarrassing, "Something for my daughter who's 14. We're from New York. We thought if you had something that said San Diego on the backside it might be cute... you know, like Victoria's Secret does on their sweatpants?"

"Hmm..." the matronly woman says, "What an unusual request... but no, we don't, at least not that I know of." And then that fateful move you hope never happens to you (especially when you're standing next to your 16 year old.) The woman, obviously a bit hard of hearing, starts yelling to the guy in the back "Hey, Ricky. Do we have any girl's underwear back there?" "Huh?" A sophisticated older man with white hair and a beard juts his head out from behind the back counter. "What did you say?" "Girl's underwear!!!" the lady says louder. And with that, my daughter glares at me as if I've committed the worst sin on the planet. "I guess we don't," she shrugs. "Sorry."

We slink out, the air thick between us. "You're so annoying," Corey finally says. "I told you not to ask for anything. I can live with what I have."

"You're annoying," I say. "I was only trying to help."

"Well I can handle things on my own. I don't need your help."

"Fine," I say.

"Fine," she says.

"Hungry?" I ask tentatively, as we pass the hotel's beachside restaurant.

"Yes," she answers just as tentatively.

"Still glad you came here with me?" I push my luck. But hey, the sun is shining.

"I guess," she says a tad reluctantly. "But next time, let's go somewhere where there's better shopping."

And for once in a very long while, we agree. Though next time, truth be told, I'd rather take my still-sweet 14 year old.

empty nesters

By Janie Lam Meyers

There is something about leaving your child, that baby once so dependent upon you, in a place where they will grow up and apart from you, that breaks your heart. The feeling is unexpected, but independence after all, is what we raise them to seek.

Our daughter, Julie, was bright, energetic, social, and very, very emotional. If something was bothering Julie, she notoriously waited until after "lights out" to remember she needed to talk with us. Be it 11:30 p.m., 12:00 midnight, 2:00 a.m., or later, she'd jump out of bed, rush into our room, turn on the light, and announce: "Oh, Mom and Dad, I forgot I needed to tell you ..."

Blinking open our eyes in the suddenly too bright room, struggling to sit up in bed, trying to wake up so we could properly focus on what was so urgent it couldn't wait until morning, Julie would begin to pour out her heart. Invariably, she'd end up telling us of a struggle at school, or of trouble with her friends, or of the upcoming cheerleading competition. Or about a boyfriend, how she worried about taking the SATs, or if her roommate next year would like her. And, what if she chose the wrong college, what if she couldn't get into a sorority, and how could she possibly make it through her freshman year without a car?

Now fully awake, my husband and I nervously glanced at each other, knowing what was to come next. Julie would finally sum up her fears and begin to cry. These were not just gentle tears, mind you, but huge, loud, sobbing, tears that could go on for hours—or so it seemed at 2:30 a.m. My husband would anxiously peer at the clock, thinking of the important business meeting he needed to attend in a few hours, and sigh, knowing full well, this witching-hour event could go on for a long time. Generally, by 4:00 a.m., she was back in bed, having talked and sobbed her fears away, contentedly asleep.

Over the years, we lovingly helped her through school fears and tears, overnight camp fears and tears, visiting-friends-far-away fears and tears, and growing up fears and tears. Soon she would be off to college, and during that final summer of Julie's youth, she generously provided us with ample reason to look forward to a "full night's sleep" ahead, in her absence.

We had previously agreed that I would be the one to take and settle Julie at college, thus allowing Dad to save his vacation days for the upcoming Parents Weekend, which would give us the opportunity to visit Julie in her new home together. We packed up her stuff and shipped it to Texas. On the big day, my husband saw us off at the Philadelphia Airport where we boarded the plane. I was to stay with Julie in a hotel close to campus the first night. We had a great time shopping for and decorating her room, met her roommate and her roommate's parents, and toured the campus. Fortunately, her roommate seemed perfectly normal and they immediately liked each other. The following night, after an evening of dinner, orientations, and social get-togethers, all of the parents departed—alone (confidently knowing we'd be returning in the morning for breakfast and a final hug). Julie and her new best friend and roommate, Michelle from California, spent their very first night in the dorm as college freshmen. There were no tears from Julie as we said "good night."

Following a quick family breakfast the next morning, the freshmen were herded onto an endless line of waiting buses, ready to escort our kids off to a leadership training camp, at a lake site, several hours away, in the beautiful Texas hill country. Julie and Michelle were 2 of the 200 chosen for this honor out of about 1500 in their freshman class. It was time to say farewell. Julie was excited and eager to get on the bus. Suddenly, I was not ready to let her go.

As I dejectedly stood on the sidewalk, the buses roared away, one after another, fading off into the distance. Farther and farther, until there was no longer a bus to which I could wave good-bye from my spot, all alone, on the barren sidewalk. I was empty. My heart actually HURT—I could feel it in my chest, beating hard. I began to cry. Not just gentle tears, mind you, but these were huge, loud, sobbing, crying tears that went on and on for hours.

I climbed into my rental car, crying. I drove to a shopping center, hoping to distract my thoughts, crying. I parked the car, and entered a lovely card and gift shop, crying. I selected a couple of cards to send to Julie, took them to the sales desk to pay, crying. The kind saleslady looked into my swollen red eyes and asked if I was all right? Bursting into fresh new tears, I told her I'd just left my child at SMU and I could not stop crying. She patted my hand and assured me I'd be OK in a couple of days—it was normal. Mortified, I returned to the car. That afternoon, as I entered the hotel, still crying, the desk clerk astutely observing the state I was in, offered to send dinner to my room, perhaps with a nice bottle of wine (whine!)? I took him up on it, spent the entire night in my hotel room, sobbing and sobbing, finally crying myself to sleep. I flew home early the next morning, my tears finally spent, and fell into my husbands' warm embrace as we acknowledged, a new chapter of our life had begun.

There is something about leaving your child, that baby once so dependent upon you, in a place where they will grow up and apart from you, that breaks your heart. The feeling is unexpected, but independence after all, is what we raise them to seek. It is perfectly OK for you to sob and cry selfishly upon this sad, sweet loss. When your tears are finally gone, you will awaken one night, and realize you have entered a new and wonderful stage of your own: the freedom to enjoy a good night's rest and the many joys of Empty Nesters!

tests

by Lenore Stoller

Twitter, what's twitter?

Several months ago, while paying a hospital visit to see my brother-in-law, everyone kept asking him the same question: "**When will you be coming home?**" My brother-in-law replied he would be released as soon as he found out his test results.

How often in your life have you replied, "I'm waiting for the test results?" That simple phrase, holds different meanings at various times in our lives.

Let's take a trip down memory lane. Each year, the elementary school I attended administered a citywide test to determine which class you would be promoted to. I somehow recall waiting for the results to see if I would be in the "one" class or the "seven" class (bottom class in the grade). Most of the time, I made it to the top class but on a few occasions, I did slip to the second or third rung.

In high school, there were midterms, finals, and Regents exams. Then in our junior year, there were the PSATs and the SATs. We waited for those test results with great anticipation, since our final score would influence our future. In college, there were countless exams and then upon receiving a master's degree, I had to write a thesis and take a comprehensive test in my area of specialization.

While attending Brooklyn and City College, my future husband and I took a blood test so we could get our marriage license and start our lives together. Thankfully, we passed that simple test and our marriage has even stood the test of time—we just celebrated our 47th anniversary.

One of the most important tests of my life was my very first road test. This test provided me with a modicum of independence, which to this day, has enabled me to travel vast distances so I can visit my children and traverse the shopping and strip malls of Long Island and Boynton Beach Florida.

Now let's fast forward to the tests we're taking now. Blood tests, stress tests, tests that are not called tests, but procedures. Echocardiograms, cardiograms, MRI's, vision tests, hearing tests, and several dozen exams with long and involved names.

As I reflect on the cycle of life, it kind of makes me wish I was back in school taking my SAT. If given the choice, I'd take that exam over a colonoscopy any day of the week.

run nana run

By Sue Levine Kupcinet ★ Yentasentiments

Joining a cause called
"Save water . . .
Drink wine."
At last, a cause
I believe in!

I am a creator of many useless, but nonetheless clever ideas. I have been many things in my lifetime . . . I guess you could say that I have a very short attention span. I started out a teacher . . . became pregnant with my daughter . . . and quit to be a stay-at-home-mom. I loved every minute of that . . . but my mind was always creating and I was forever at my, excuse the expression, typewriter. I wrote and published *Chicago Gourmet* a restaurant guidebook in Chicago. I wrote many children's books . . . just never had them published, so they are now all squished into a file cabinet where everything was stored before computer memory.

After I became pregnant with my second child, I created the idea of sibling T-shirts. I wanted my daughter to be included in my pregnancy, so they started out with "I'm going to be a big sister/brother." Then after the birth of my son, I created "I love my big sister/baby brother" shirts. These evolved into the now famous "I am the big brother...little sister" shirts that are everywhere. But alas, they are not mine. I thought I was so clever and interviewed with *Woman's Wear Daily* all about the shirts ... and, oops, they were ripped-off by a large company.

As my kids got older, I opened a store of fun but unnecessary items called "Splurge." It was like my third child ... I loved every minute I was there. I found "Judy," a very talented seamstress and created the personalized soft sculpture Emmy and Oscar. It became my best seller ... People were coming in to order them and calls came from all over the country. Life was good until one day I received two letters. One was from the TV academy and one from the film academy ordering me to cease and desist. They obviously had no sense of humor!

The birth of my next idea came shortly after I received the first letter my daughter sent me from overnight camp. It read,

Dear Mom,

"If you love me at all, you'll come take me home."

I was booking my flight when my husband talked me out of going. I had such a strong desire to put my arms around her and tell her everything would be OK. Aha ... A hug! I needed to send her a hug. I ran to my typewriter ... OK, OK, I still had my Smith Corona and started to create the "Long Distance Hug." Wow ... this was it. It's the perfect gift for birthdays, get well, anything. Everyone needs a hug ... it's the next best thing to being there. I called "Judy" who got to work sewing up soft sculpture arms that locked with Velcro. I designed and printed 1000 long distance hug boxes to start. Creativity is one thing ... business sense is another. Today, I have 960 boxes in my garage. You're probably thinking I sold 40 ... wrong. I used 40 to send out eBay purchases.

Nothing stopped me. I developed a board game that was ripped off by a major toy company. I developed it into a game show that is out there now. What are the chances?

The good news is my kids grew up, my daughter married, and soon I had my first grandchild. The bad news is they lived in Chicago and I live in Los Angeles. I spent my first year flying out to see this precious new addition to my life. My days started by hearing any news about Sam and I thought about him all day long. My mind seemed to stop being creative. A good friend asked me to proofread a book she was writing about a very serious subject. It was about the death of her daughter. We would meet and go through her latest chapter over lunch or dinner. One night, we met at a Mexican restaurant on a very busy well-lit street. We sat near the window. Both of us were grandmothers and age was starting to set in. This time it was going to work to our advantage. Neither of us could see a thing without our glasses. We saw a store across the street and we both squinted to see the name. Yenta Tattoos. Could that be? We got hysterical. We put away her book and took out a notepad and started writing down funny tattoos that a Yenta would have. The more we wrote, the more we laughed. Later we found out it was called "Yonni Tattoos." Close enough! After weeks of writing Yenta Tattoos we started to wonder what in the hell we could do with these. We didn't want to give them up so we decided to transform them into greeting cards and that's how Yenta Sentiments was born. I felt like Grandma Moses. We were starting a new business at our age when we were supposed to be knitting and passing around photos of our grandkids. Today we still enjoy creating our funny cards and have licensed out to a major company. We actually write for them, too.

I still feel like I can do anything. However, now I have four grandchildren and they have proved me wrong! When they come to visit, I have a chart crossing off the days until they arrive. By day two, I have a private chart marking off the days, hours, minutes, and seconds until they leave! They say grandkids keep you young. Please, God, tell me there's an easier way!

It's the hardest work I've ever done. I went to stay with them when their parents went away on vacation. The oldest was five and the youngest was two months old and not sleeping through the night. I said ... sure I'll do that. There's a nanny so no problem. The first day seemed like four weeks had passed. I finally had them all in their pajamas, when the nanny yelled up the stairs, "Good night ... I'll be back in the morning around nine." I had never experienced panic before. I started to shake. I broke out in a sweat ... and then I cried! Yes. I did.

I learned a lesson. Some things are too much for me. I made it through that week barely and spent the next four in bed at home. I remember that I'm older, wiser and exhausted, so ...

See Nana Run.

Run Nana Run.

Who am I kidding? Walk Nana Walk ... and don't look back!

the sanitation mom

by Beth Feldman ★ Role Mommy

At ball field for several hours with no snacks in sight. Will tweet for food.

Can someone explain to me why I am the human trash can in my family? It's not like I've volunteered for the job but somehow, when my kids are finished with their gum, their drinks or their tissues, they don't hold onto their refuse. Oh no. Why do that when you have the Sanitation Mom sitting directly in front, chauffeuring them around from one activity to another?

Picture the scene. We're running late, as usual and I've given the kids a quick snack so they won't complain that they're famished the minute we hit the open road. Within one minute and forty five seconds one of them has finished their juice box and granola bar and I can feel little fingers tapping me on my shoulder as I'm trying to make a right turn.

"Mommy, here's my garbage. Take it."

I don't know when I became the wastebasket but even when my husband is around, they instantly hand me their half eaten snacks so that I can magically make the garbage disappear. And when we're outside of the car, my role as Sanitation Mom kicks in at movie theaters, festivals, museums, the zoo, there is not a place in the tri-state area that I haven't traversed where my kids have used me to get rid of their trash.

Sometimes, if I've tried to ignore my kids while they've attempted to hand me a half eaten yodel or Juicy Juice while we're cruising down the Hutchinson River Pkwy, I've lived to suffer severe consequences. One year, my daughter decided to use my $300 Michael Kors bag as a trash receptacle. And when I almost experienced a "Mommy Dearest" moment when I saw her YooHoo dripping into my supple leather designer tote, she looked at me squarely in the eye and said "Well mommy, if you had taken my garbage when I asked you to, this never would have happened."

Now I know I should just tell them, it's your garbage, you find a place to dispose of it, but frankly it's just easier to take care of the mess rather than let something smelly fester in the back seat of my minivan. And besides, at least I know I'm not alone in my garbage duties. There are other parents who have become voluntary sanitation workers, too.

Just yesterday, I was in the supermarket on the check out line standing next to a sweet looking three year old savoring a piece of mozzarella cheese on a toothpick. As his dad was busy packing up their groceries and paying the cashier, the tyke held out the toothpick while motioning to his dad. When his father didn't pay attention to his directive to relieve him of the toothpick, the whining began to commence.

"Daddy . . . take this away!" he whined. And within one second, the dad grabbed the toothpick and proceeded to drop it on the same conveyer belt where my produce and Weight Watchers frozen dinners were about to be deposited. Now that is just plain offensive. If you have accepted the role of Sanitation Mom or Dad it is your obligation to dispose of all waste in a trash receptacle. If you can't live up to the demands of the job, then you must instruct your child that they must hold onto said toothpick until they can find a trash can themselves and drop it where it belongs.

I never realized there's a code of Sanitation Mom ethics, but there is. Just like the tell-tale phrase, you break it, you pay, the same holds true for garbage. They give you their trash, you throw it out. And if you break the rules, then maybe your kid can take on garbage duty themselves. And if you believe that will ever happen, I have a bridge to sell you in Brooklyn.

type b mom

by Liz Gumbinner ★ Mom 101

Heading to a vegetarian dinner/cooking demo and am terrified I'll have carnivore Tourette's and start yelling MEAT! MEAT! at random moments

I like the idea of being the really buttoned-up Type A germaphobe mom; you know, that parent who takes the time to do things like disinfect the laundry basket and throw away that one pancake instead of just plucking the dog hair off of it. Those moms always seem just so caring. So utterly concerned with the well-being of their children.

What a very nice thing to seem to be.

I did experiment with germaphobia briefly, back in those sleepless early days of motherhood when we all decide what kind of mom we think we will be.

When my daughter was old enough to beg for swing-set time, I diligently toted both her and my travel packs of hand sanitizer to the playground on weekends. I made sure to squirt goopy dime-sized blobs into her palm for all the world to see. And then swung my diaper bag behind one shoulder and stood proud and tall and I waited. I waited for some sort of grand reaction, some nod of approval or secret wink from my breeding Brooklyn sisters, cross-legged on the benches with the perfect hair and the oddly clean Bugaboos. I waited for some acceptance into their uber-caring Type A Mom Club (the one with the germ-free secret handshake).

Nothing.

Not an iota of public adulation for my loving attention to antibacterial hand sanitization. It was confounding.

That's when I realized I was simply not one of them. I would never belong to that club, no matter how much I faked it. There is something about me that just shouts Type B Mom.

The reality is, I'm just as happy to pluck my girls from the sandbox, rinse off their hands in the water fountain like the dads do, and call it a day. I am happy to subscribe to the "a little dirt won't hurt" school of parenting also known as What Doesn't Kill You Makes Your Immune System Stronger or So I Tell Myself When I'm Scraping Crud Out of The Sippy Top Lid with My Nails.

I'm late for pediatrician appointments. I can't make straight parts in my girls' hair. I forget to send them in the snow with hats, as the kind sanctimommies of the neighborhood are delighted to point out with their eyebrows raised as far as Botox will allow. And if you're bringing your own baby to our apartment, don't expect anything close to childproofing around here. Our cabinet door latches actually remain unopened inside a cabinet. Which one, I'm not entirely sure.

I mean to do all these things, really I do. But every day that Thalia and Sage are still here, healthy and happy enough to chase each other around the house with forest green magic markers yelling, "STOP DRAWING ON ME! MOMMY SHE DRAWED ON ME!" I figure I'm doing OK.

What's funny is that in most accounts, I should be a Type A Mom. (Dammit.) I've been a Type A Person the better part of my adult life. There was a time not so long ago that I was doing daily battle at a frenetic ad agency, juggling conference calls and editing sessions and occasional bouts of clever headline writing all with perfectly manicured toes. I managed my calendar, I balanced my checkbook, ate before I got shaky. I had it down.

And yet somehow all that Type A somehow flew out of my uterus at New York Presbyterian along with my firstborn. I can't entirely explain it. And I don't try to fight it.

Perhaps it has to do with the fact that I am a working mom and there's just not enough Type A to go around to every part of my life. One can only be frantic in so many places.

Or occasionally I wonder if maybe there isn't a teeny bit of Type A lying dormant within my cells, just waiting to spring to life and . . . I don't know, organize something. Maybe a splashy school fundraiser or a gluten-free organic bake sale. You know, for orphans.

But for now I'm happy just to be the mom of happy kids with dirty noses who say "thank you" and "please" and get to eat ice cream before dinner on warm spring afternoons.

One day, I hope they'll forgive me for it.

to clean or not to clean?

by Jenny Baitch Isenman ★ Suburban Jungle

Does anyone else think the Power Puff Girls need Brazilian waxes to wear skirts that short?

To clean, or not to clean? One mom debates the age-old question that has beleaguered mothers since the dawn of time.

I remember the days before I found a regular housekeeper... I cleaned a lot! In fact, I could do nothing else around my house until it was clean. I would clean in the morning, watch my kids immediately undo my work, and then clean the same stuff all over again. I would start at 9 a.m. when they went to school, and then again at 9 p.m. when they went to bed. Each time I was amazed at how long it took to clean the house, and how quickly it became undone.

I made up fascinating "cleaning games" to justify not spending time playing Nerf dart tag, or doing spin art like the "good Mommies" did. Our play was much more educational ... I honed my son's eye for detail and fine motor skills: "Jake, let's see if you can match the socks and roll them neatly into pairs." I knew he was a true genius the day he found matches for the 23 mate-less socks I had been re-washing for a year. I taught my daughter about the nuances of tone and hue: "Ryan, which colors are dark and which are light?" "Honey that shirt may be white, but the stripes are red. That's a major oversight on your part. I hope you weren't hungry because that just cost you dinner."

I considered asking my husband for help, but the truth is, to watch him try and clean could send us straight to divorce court. He would say, "Just do it once a day, why waste your time?" Which, by the way, is the same argument he has for oral hygiene, so who could listen to him? If you want the job done right, i.e. your way . . . , you have to do it yourself.

I couldn't delegate because I was too disappointed in the way someone would load my dishwasher. Loading a dishwasher takes serious problem-solving skills and visual prowess; done correctly, it is an algorithm of perfectly fitting pieces with not a single one to spare. OK, I'm beginning to sound pathetic, but some of you actually get what I'm saying. You know who you are, you're the ones thinking, "Please, my dish loading could kick your ass . . . Bitch!" Well, you know what I say? Bring it!

I was so vehemently against having help because I was sure it would reflect on some inability to be a good Mother/Housewife (a title I never thought I would covet the way that I do). I also convinced myself that having help would weaken my right to be a martyr. However, my need to have "a life" and to resent my husband less won out, and I hired someone.

After a single day I felt like screaming "FREEDOM!" while swooshing down a mountain with a cool breeze on my face, or into a deep echoing canyon while blowing my Riccola horn . . . but, alas, Florida is flat. So I traipsed into the lake (swamp) in our back yard, and screamed at the top of my lungs. Unfortunately, it was "ALLIGATOR" and not "FREEDOM," but I feel my point was made. As soon as I zigzagged back into my house, I considered all of my options: Grocery shop, get Starbucks with a friend, shop for my kids, go to the gym, go back to the grocery store to pick up anything I forgot the first time around, or get Starbucks again. My days were filled with endless monotony and it was exhilarating. My afternoons were completely open. I could do all kinds of things while my daughter napped. I could eat a late lunch, go to the gym, get Starbucks, get more groceries, shower. When my son got home we played Nerf dart tag and did spin art. Of course some days I was too full from all the lunching and Starbucks, so we lazed on the sofa together and watched Sponge Bob.

Each day I returned to a neat and straightened house, with clean clothes and an organized pantry. I began saying things that gave away control like, "You know, I don't care if you rearrange my drawers, whatever is easier for you." I had to make phone calls to find out where my daughter's stuffed kitty and my new Hogan bag were, and I reveled in it. My exciting monotony was getting boring, not to mention expensive, so I decided I would have to do something to distract me from spending money. I tried chewing gum. No luck. I tried reading. I read books by Dr. Oz and Dr. Drew and Dr. Phil. I even read a lovely memoir by Dr. J. All to no avail.

So, I decided to write again. Three weeks later, I felt

reborn and my Amex felt dejected, jumping out of my bag anytime we so much as drove past a retail store. It would even put extra groceries in my cart when I wasn't looking. My Amex, however, wasn't the only one let down. A week later my housekeeper told me she was offered a job at a physical therapist's office. I said, "Are you kidding me? Who do you expect to do my laundry, clean the kitty litter, the dog pee, the garage ... me? I had that job once, it sucked!" Luckily, when I talk fast she doesn't understand a word. Then I slowly said "You have to take it, congratulations!" and gave her a huge hug. She still comes about five hours a week because in her own words, "I'll help as much as I can. I know how much you need me." Apparently, she's never seen me load a dishwasher, but if you don't tell, I won't either.

airing my dirty laundry

by Lenore Stoller

I've just joined a new Facebook group. Bubbes who blog.

As a parent, we seldom notice how quickly time goes by. We seem to forget that our children are not only growing taller, but are moving rapidly from kindergarten to college and before you know it, they have left the nest. Or so we think.

I really didn't think about it much until our son headed off to SUNY at Albany. He had not done exceedingly well during his high school years, preferring to party rather than study. He spent that first semester close to home at Brooklyn College and managed to pull a 4.0 GPA. As a result, Albany accepted him as a transfer student without any conditions whatsoever. So in the middle of January, my husband packed his used Oldsmobile Cutlass Supreme with everything Eric, our son, could possibly need and followed him up to Albany so he could start the semester in style. We bought everything you could imagine to make his transition to living on his own as comfortable as possible.

As Eric departed, I suddenly felt very sad and lonely—wondering how I would manage to be separated from our first child. Our daughter was still at home and I was very thankful that at least I had one child to look after on a daily basis. The first week was really tough for me. I still cooked for four of us and called Eric every evening. Friday night of the first week arrived, the doorbell rang, and lo-and-behold our son had come home! Was he homesick? Did he miss my home cooking? Eric came into the house dragging a rather large garbage bag behind him. I was puzzled—but our returning son smiled and said "I brought my dirty laundry." Wow! What a gift! I did his laundry and spent the weekend preparing snacks and goodies for his return trip to school.

Once again, I spent the week really missing our eldest child, but by the time Friday rolled around again, who returned home to the nest but our beloved son with an even larger garbage bag with all of his dirty laundry. By the time he was ready to drive back to school, I was exhausted—washing, ironing, folding, and packing all the stuff Eric had brought home with him. We kissed him good-bye the second weekend and I collapsed on the couch—not sure if I missed him or if I was just exhausted from his "gift."

The third Friday rolled around and you guessed it, Eric returned home with an even larger garbage bag of dirty laundry. I took care of this load, but I had finally reached the limit of my patience. In other words, I had had it! Empty-nest syndrome or not, this had to stop. So I informed my son that from now on, I was giving him some extra cash so he could take his dirty clothes to the laundromat. Without missing a beat, I handed him a box of detergent, a written list of instructions on how to operate a washing machine and dryer and informed him that he should stay at school on weekends, join in the social scene, and instead of driving home, he should use the time he spent driving to study. Boy! What a novel idea! And after he drove off that February afternoon, armed with industrial strength detergent that could wash 64 loads of clothes, Eric finally stopped bringing home his dirty laundry. Instead, within two weeks, he found himself a girlfriend. Want to know where they met? The laundromat.

the final addition

by Beth Feldman ★ Role Mommy

How bad could sheet-rocking be anyway? Famous last words.

When I reflect upon the most harried moments of my life, while birth definitely takes top honors, cleaning up after an extensive home renovation comes in at a close second. A few years ago, my husband and I were itching to move. With two kids and two cats, we had outgrown our three-bedroom, one-and-1/2 bath, 1950's starter house, and to be perfectly honest, I was secretly plotting for years to find the center hall colonial of our dreams. After combing through the *New York Times* Real Estate section, we happened upon a house a few blocks away that was for sale by owner, and when we checked it out it was love at first sight. Even though the house was missing a garage, you had to walk through the master bedroom to get to the nursery, and there seemed to be a distinct musty smell that followed us as we took a tour of the ground floor and basement, I was ready to pack my bags and move into that picturesque 1930's colonial.

Meanwhile, in the span of one weekend, we spruced up our starter home, placed a "For Sale by Owner" ad in the paper and managed to land a buyer within a few days. But, not so fast. Just as we were riding high thinking we were well on our way to our second home, the first owner got cold feet and the couple who wanted to buy our place tried to re-negotiate. Unbeknownst to us, their deal-seeking father-in-law trailed the home inspector, thinking he'd be able to shave a few thousand dollars off the asking price once the inspection report revealed we had to replace our 50-year-old boiler and a portion of the roof. As he inspected the foundation, while simultaneously nodding his head in disgust, I gave that man the nastiest look I could muster while shooting him a telepathic warning; Back off Bob Vila!

So, there we were, sitting in our den, annoyed that a meddling in-law was throwing a monkey wrench into our plans, when our neighbor invited us over to take a look at their home renovation. Since we had the same style house as theirs, we were curious to see how we could transform our place without ever having to pack our bags. When we stepped inside the front door, we were completely blown away. My eyes were blinded by the gleaming granite countertops, Viking stove, and cherry wood cabinets in their expansive kitchen. Their three bedrooms were turned into five, the cozy family room now included a gas fireplace with a mahogany mantel, and the bathrooms had the most gorgeous basket-weave marble tile I had ever set my sights on. From that moment forward, we decided we were going to get ourselves an architect and perform our very own Extreme Home Makeoverx on our 1950's Rob and Laura Petrie split.

Since I like doing things at warp speed, I instantly found the perfect architect who incorporated all the design ideas I had given him. After eavesdropping on prospective buyers at our Open House who had complained the dining room was too small and there weren't enough bathrooms or closets, we decided we were going to expand the dining room, add a sunroom and mudroom, knock down our one-car garage to make room for two, and build the master suite of our dreams.

Lucky for us, one of the best contractors in our neighborhood was set to begin construction on our neighbor's house across the street, so we made a deal to have him start work on our house immediately after they were finished. Before we knew it, Lars Jackson and his crew of merry construction men moved the port-o-san over to our lawn and 12 workers (who soon became my fast friends) stepped inside and began to dismantle our house.

Most sane people who add 1,200 square feet to their homes usually move out for a few months to spare themselves the aggravation of being surrounded by dirt, debris, dust and destruction, but not the Feldman's. As part of my 'day job' as a mom blogger and parenting expert, I've been fortunate enough to work with Swiffer, so when it comes to cleaning I know just what it takes to get the job done. Armed with a Swiffer WetJet and a case-load of Antibacterial cleaning solution, I was ready to tackle anything the construction crew threw my way. Knock down my one car garage and my favorite lilac bush? No problem. Rip through walls and tear down a staircase so you can build a new one? Piece of cake. Bang incessantly from 7:30 a.m. until 5 p.m. as I try to listen in on a conference call? That's what the mute button is for. No matter what construction curve ball they threw at me, I was ready for anything—until the drywall commenced.

You see, the funny thing about a home renovation is that the demolition only takes a few days. Then, they framed the rooms, started laying down floors, install plumbing and electrical and the remaining jobs that seem to last an eternity and drive you to drink heavily is the drywall, painting, and tile work.

Let's start with the drywall. When we started our renovation, people kept warning me about that part of the project. With ominous voices they'd warn, "Just wait for the drywall." Cavalier about the whole construction process, I'd shrug and say, "Oh, it'll be fine—we've handled it pretty well so far. How bad could sheet-rocking be anyway?" Famous last words.

The problem with drywall is that once it's hammered into that wood frame and you hire a painter to sand it down and get it primed and ready for your palette of Benjamin Moore country colonials, you're already of the mind-set that your project is almost finished. Except it's not. In fact, when you're on the construction locomotive and they install new walls in your home, as much as you want to jump off that train, you can't. And so, you're subjected to sanding, a process by which tiny particles of dust fill the room in swirls above your head. Within seconds, those swirls land on everything in its wake, including your entertainment center (that was only partially covered in sheets), your brand new hardwood floors, your two cats, and your unsuspecting kids. Before we knew it, our home resembled a scene right out of White Christmas, except it was July and we were Jewish. I know it needed to be cleaned, but I didn't even know where to begin. I spent the better part of my evening Swiffer-ing like a madwoman and I have to admit, part of me never thought we would be able to enjoy the television again, or walk barefoot on our once-gleaming hardwood floors. After wiping down the floors and climbing precariously onto one of my couches to reach the top of my uncovered entertainment center, I threw my two kids into a bath and watched the cats lick dust out of their fur. Thankfully, we had survived our bout with drywall, but weren't out of the woods just yet.

One of the most exciting parts of our renovation was the master bathroom suite I conjured up in my mind after visiting several incredible hotel boudoirs, stealing some design tips along the way. I spent the better part of my summer visiting tile stores throughout Westchester County. On my quest to find the perfect colors for my masterpiece, I managed to track down a reasonably priced pure white Thassos marble tile at Ideal Tile in Yonkers, while I set my sights on mosaics that were on the other side of town at Artistic Tile in White Plains. Further complicating matters, I found my Celeste Blue marble countertop at Marble America in New Rochelle and then drove to Masterpiece Tile a few blocks away to pick out our Ming Green and Celeste Blue chic-let mosaic tiles along with bull-nosed borders. Yes, I was insane, but I was a woman on a quest to create the perfect bathroom. During the summer of my final addition, I managed to not only befriend several construction workers, an electrician and plumber who were all named John, but two friendly tile men named Wasiim and Salaam. As we chatted about world peace and the future of the Middle East, I managed to haggle and negotiate some pretty reasonable rates from my two favorite tile store owners. During one nerve-wracking afternoon, I even convinced Wasiim to bull-nose a few tiles on the spot when my temperamental tile man informed me we needed those tiles immediately or else work on my bathroom would come to a grinding halt.

And, speaking of grinding halt—Gino, my tile guy, decided to take a three-week sojourn to Italy just as we were about to finish what I fondly refer to as The Palace. Just as all my tiles were ready and waiting for Gino in my brand new two-car garage, he had mysteriously disappeared. Of course, had we checked the passenger list on Alitalia, we would have known that Gino takes an annual summer trip with his family to Southern Italy. As we begged Lars to send out a Sicilian search party for Gino, he calmed our frazzled nerves and assured us he'd return to finish the job. After his respite, Gino was in a Zen-like state. With a cigarette stub dangling out of the corner of his mouth, he began laying tile as if he had been possessed by the spirit of Michelangelo. Perhaps Gino received some divine inspiration during that Italian vacation, but all I can say is he created the bathroom to end all bathrooms and to this day, when I take people upstairs to see The Palace, it literally takes their breath away.

As I now sit in my sunroom reflecting on that hectic summer of drywall, I have to admit I am so happy we never moved. Our little home was transformed into the split colonial of my dreams that I plan to enjoy for many years to come with my husband, kids, two cats, and two hermit crabs. Just as I grew up in the same house where I was born, I'm looking forward to seeing my own children create lasting memories in a home filled with love, laughter and countless bathroom tours.

author bios

Beth Feldman is the founder of RoleMommy.com, an online community and events company dedicated to inspiring, entertaining, and empowering today's busy moms to pursue their passion while raising a family. Feldman is a former television-network executive who pole vaulted off the corporate ladder to become the president of her own PR consulting agency, and she's the host of Blog Talk Radio's brand new Role Mommy Radio network. Beth is the co-author of *Peeing in Peace: Tales & Tips for Type A Moms* (Sourcebooks) and is a contributor to the new bestseller *True Mom Confessions* (Penguin).

Tracy Beckerman writes the syndicated humor column, LOST IN SUBURBIA, which is carried by over 400 newspapers nationally in 25 states and read by more than 3.5 million people. She is also the author of the book, *Rebel without a Minivan: Observations on Life in the 'Burbs,* a collection of her essays, which was published last year. Prior to writing her column, Tracy worked in the television industry, creating award-winning promos for such clients as CBS, NBC, and Lifetime Television. In 2007, she was selected as an Erma Bombeck Humor Writer of the Month for her essays on motherhood and suburban life. Tracy has appeared on NBC's *Today Show* and the CBS *Early Show* and is currently hard at work on her second book. She is also developing a sitcom Web series based on her column. Tracy lives in New Providence, NJ with her husband and two children, dog, lizard, and chinchilla. She is only responsible for feeding three of them.

Beth Blecherman started her career in application development, system auditing, and then Senior Manager, Computer Process Integrity, for Deloitte. After senior management, she decided to take on family management and started blogging as her career 2.0. She is a co-founder of the Silicon Valley Moms Group, collaborative mom blogs in regions across the country, as well as the first international site: Canada Moms Blog. Blecherman founded TechMamas.com, a tech blog with a parenting slant, as a platform to discuss technology and gadgets for families. She also consults with companies on blogger outreach and social media strategies.

Ciaran Blumenfeld is a writer, designer, and creative social media consultant. She is the creator of the "Francie Pants" children's clothing line and is the owner/editor of Popshopology.com (dedicated to retail therapy) and Carand Caboodle (dedicated to family travel and transportation). Ciaran is the proud mom of four deeply unique and different children who have humbled and taught her so much over the years, while keeping her constantly on her toes. She loves all her children dearly, even when they make an ungodly mess and teach her that she does not know it all, after all. She also still loves Thai food, despite the incident included in this book.

Melissa Chapman and her brood of three live in the urban concrete jungle of NYC. When she's not busy putting someone in a time-out, stepping on action figures, hand-feeding her dog/child or braiding hair, she's trying to find indulgences that remind her of her prekid days when she felt sexy and no one ever called her ma'am! But above all else, she has taken a solemn vow to never under any circumstances succumb to slipping on a pair of mom jeans! She contributes to *Time Out NY Kids* and iVillage, writes a blog called "This mom wouldn't be caught dead wearing mom jeans," and a weekly column for the *Staten Island Advance*.

Danielle Dardashti is the Integrated Sales Manager for Meredith Video Solutions, the division of Meredith Corporation that creates Parents TV. Previously, she ran the sales department at Connect with Kids. She is an Emmy award-winning former on-air television reporter, a published author of three books for parents and educators, has produced critically-acclaimed television documentaries, and has written parenting articles for national magazines. Danielle lives in White Plains, NY with her husband Roni Sarig, and their children Uri and Raquel.

Vanessa Druckman is a freelance writer, blogger, and mother to three little monsters. She just relocated to Ohio from New Jersey with her family, having only begun to own up to being a Jersey Girl, a label she never imagined having grown up in France. She blogs about cooking and parenting at www.chefdruck.com.

Nancy Friedman was an award-winning freelance television writer and producer for such clients as HBO, Lifetime and Nickelodeon until she decided to stop making money and start writing. Her humor essays have been syndicated in the online versions of *The Miami Herald*, *The Sacramento Bee*, *The Fresno Bee*, and *The Charlotte Observer*, among others. Nancy has ghost-written two books on interior design, and her work has appeared in the anthologies *The Knitter's Gift*, (Adams Media, 2004) and *The Bigger the Better the Tighter the Sweater* (Seal Press, 2007). She is a contributor to NYCMomsblog.com, and TravelingMom.com. FromHipto Housewife.com is her blog about momming, aging, and her twenty year quest to lose the same ten pounds. She lives in

NYC with her husband and boy/girl twins.

Andrea Forstadt lives on Long Island, NY and is the mom of four, including one-year-old identical twin boys (who, she was told, were supposed to be identical twin girls; you'll have to wait for that story in the sequel).

Sara R. Fisher is an off-ramped mother of a toddler-aged son living in Chicago. A former employee-relations consultant, Sara now spends her days scheduling play dates, maximizing nap time, and trying to use the adult side of her brain every once in awhile. A burgeoning writer, Sara's work has been published in *Chicago Parent* magazine, the *Washington Post*'s On Balance blog, Babble.com, and her blog, selfmademom.net.

Liz Gumbinner is the voice of the popular parenting blog Mom-101 which has been featured in *The New York Times* and called "funny some of the time" by an enthusiastic anonymous commenter. She's also the co-founder of the shopping and design blog Cool Mom Picks. Her humorous (some of the time) take on parenting can be found in magazines like *Brain, Child*, and *New York Parent*, and in the books *Sleep Is for the Weak*, *True Mom Confessions*, and *42 Rules for Working Moms*.

Jenny Baitch Isenman is a freelance humor writer, wiper of tushies, noses, and countertops...not in that order. She has two beautiful, amazing, perfect children who always do and say the right things. She has written for local and national magazines. She currently writes for multiple sites including, iVillage.com, NewParent.com, CityMommy.com, and JewishTimes.com. She has a hilariously funny and relatable blog called Suburban Jungle.net. She guarantees that reading it will make you tanner, smarter, and reduces cellulite.

Meredith Jacobs is the author of *The Modern Jewish Mom's Guide to Shabbat* (HarperCollins), host of the radio show Connecting Family (WYPR-FM), and the television show *Modern Jewish Mom* (The Jewish Channel). She lives in Rockville, MD with husband Jonathan, daughter Sofie, son Jules, insane-dog Mac, and a tank of seahorses. Sofie survived the traumatic incident revealed in her mom's essay and went on to co-author a book with Meredith titled: *Just Between Us: A Journal for Mothers and Daughters* (Chronicle Books, Spring 2010).

Sue Levine Kupcinet is a teacher, creator of many items, published author with Simon and Schuster *Chicago Gourmet*, co-owner of "Yenta Sentiments" greeting cards, wife of 41 years, mother of two and grandmother of four.

Cheryl Lage is the author of *Twinspiration: Real-Life Advice from Pregnancy through the First Year* (2006, Taylor Trades) She is a part-time producer, a freelance writer/editor and a full-time mom. Her perspectives on family life have appeared in a wide array of print, Web, and broadcast media including: *USA Today, Good Housekeeping*, *Pregnancy*, *TWINS*, Parents.com, People's Celebrity Baby Blog, and many, many more. Currently, Cheryl lives with her family in Richmond, VA and blogs daily at twinfatuation.com.

Sherry Shealy Martschink has had a varied career, from state senator to clown. Or perhaps that's not so varied at all! She has been a member of the SC House of Representatives, of a local school board, and of the SC State Senate. After losing a race for lieutenant governor, she became SC Workers' Compensation Commissioner for 12 years. Sherry has been a teacher, a radio talk-show host, and a pianist in clubs and restaurants. At the age of 54, she entered law school, graduating at 57. Most remarkable, all three of her children Tiffany, Tree, and Mandy survived having her as a mother and are now grown and successful in their own areas. Sherry is now a motivational/inspirational speaker, writer, and consultant. Her blog is "EX Marks the Spot" at www.blondesherry.blogspot.com. She also teaches tap dancing to students who are "at least 50 years old."

Issa M. Mas is a native New Yorker and an advocate for Single Moms everywhere. She currently writes a column for www.Examiner.com about family events in New York City. A passion for writing began early for Issa; she was presented her first award for a piece of her writing at only seven years old by then-New York City Mayor Edward Koch as a city-wide winner of a poetry contest. Issa is a published poet, writer of children's books, blogger (Single Mama NYC), and founder of www.YourSingleParenting.com—a resource website for all single parents.

Jenna McCarthy is an internationally-published writer and the author of *The Parent Trip: From High Heels and Parties to Highchairs and Potties*, and *Cheers to the New Mom/Dad*! Her work has appeared in more than 50 magazines, on dozens of websites, and in several anthologies including the popular Chicken Soup series. She has held staff positions for leading publishers in New York and Los Angeles, and for two years served as the co-host of the top-rated KTYD *Early Show*. She lives in lovely Santa Barbara, CA, where she enjoys sculpting Play-Doh and watching the value of her home plummet. Jenna currently is hard at work on her next project, a practical guide to living with and continuing to love the TV-addicted, sex-obsessed, listening-impaired Neanderthal you married. In her spare time, she wonders what she used to do with all of her spare time. Visit her online at www.jennamccarthy.com.

Dawn Meehan grew up in Chicago where she began her writing career at the age of five with her widely praised, "The Lucky Leprechaun," an epic tale of a leprechaun who was yes, you guessed it, lucky. Dawn has six children, basically because she didn't want seven. She is the author of "Because I Said So" and spends her days blogging at BecauseISaidSo.com, changing diapers, cleaning pudding off her ceiling, tackling insurmountable piles of laundry, and explaining to her kids why they can't have a pet squirrel or an indoor slip-n-slide.

Janie Lam Meyers grew up, married, and raised her family in suburban Philadelphia, PA. She currently lives with her husband, Gene, in Charlotte, NC, where they take pleasure in "empty nesting." They are the proud parents of three grown daughters, a son-in-law, and three grandchildren. She enjoys a part-time career in sales and marketing, taking writing courses, and being an author. She is currently working on her first fiction novel.

Jeanne Muchnick is a multitasking mama who's been writing about her two girls ever since they were in utero. She's the former Editor of *Baby Magazine* turned freelancer whose parenting stories have appeared in a variety of national and local magazines including *The New York Times*, *The Boston Globe*, *Woman's Day*, *Ladies' Home Journal*, *Parents*, *Parenting*, *Pregnancy*, *Women's Health & Fitness*, *FamilyFun*, *InTown Magazine*, *The Daily News*, *Westchester Magazine*, and more. She has also contributed to momlogic.com, momcentral.com, travelingmom.com, and sprout.com, though she admits she's still "old-fashioned" and prefers reading/writing for magazines. She lives in Larchmont, NY with her two (now teenage and embarrassed to be with her) daughters, her husband Mark, and her shedding (and annoying) flat-coated retriever, Chip. When she's not writing, you can find her doing the aundry, picking up the dry cleaning, food shopping, vacuuming, and stocking up on red wine.

Abby Pecoriello was so busy hot gluing rhinestones onto her front door that she almost totally forgot to write her bio for this book. But serendipitously, she ran out of glue sticks and rushed onto her computer to order more (they don't sell the really sticky ones in stores, you have to get them online!) While on her computer, Beth pinged her and said "I need your bio by tomorrow mama!" So she's writing it right now. I am, I mean, Abby is the Site Director of Nickelodeon's ParentsConnect.com and author of *Crafty Mama Makes 49 Fast, Fabulous and Foolproof (baby & Toddler) Projects*. When she's not crafting or websiting, she's putting on musicals or shopping for cute leggings with her daughters, Lily and Sasha. Oh yeah, her hubby, Mike, loves musicals too, but he doesn't wear cute leggings.

Eden Pontz is Executive Producer at CNN's New York Bureau in addition to her position of "Mama In-Chief" at home. An award-winning journalist, she's produced and reported domestically and internationally. Sadly, she moved from London back to New York just before giving birth—nixing her daughter's chance for dual citizenship, but increasing her potential post-college job struggle and need for therapy. She lives in Brooklyn, NY with her husband and toddler daughter because she felt the need to confront her fear of bridges and tunnels every day. Eden writes for NYC Moms Blog as well as contributing to cnn.com. And she continues running. Because after all, isn't life all about the chase?

Jen Singer is the mother of two boys who talk to her through the bathroom door. She is the creator of MommaSaid.net, the back fence of the Internet, and a Forbes Best of the Web community for moms. She is the author of the Stop Second Guessing Yourself parenting guides (HCI) and *You're a Good Mom (and Your Kids Aren't So Bad Either)* (Sourcebooks). Named one of Swiffer's first Amazing Women of the Year, she is a Huggies PULL-UPS Potty Training Partner and has served as a spokesperson for SC Johnson's Nature's Source, Coinstar, and Hershey's. She has appeared dozens of radio and television programs.

A soccer coach, class mom, and cancer survivor, she lives in northern New Jersey with her husband and two tween sons who leave various rolling objects on the floor of her minivan for her to discover whenever she hits the brakes.

Lenore Stoller is a grandmother of three, mom of two, devoted wife, and Role Mommy of the Millenium. She is a retired deputy superintendent and adjunct professor who now spends her days tap dancing, reading, doing yoga, dining with friends, doting on her grandchildren, and attending Weight Watcher meetings. She is also the mom of author Beth Feldman and contributes to RoleMommy.com under the pseudonym "Role Bubbe."

April Welch, CPO is a Certified Professional Organizer residing in central Washington state with her husband and two young children. She has been a professional organizer for several years and has been instinctively organizing most of her adult life. Her organizing specialties are with children/families and the chronic disorganized communities. While her philosophies are centered on how individuals are "wired" she believes in providing a fun and educational environment with simple solutions to all organizing dilemmas. She offers live workshops, in-home consultations, virtual organizing, tele-classes, habit assessments, virtual clutter support groups, public speaking, and most recently a radio show online. April is the Franklin Covey Family Organizing Guru and the creator of Purchase with a Purpose Challenge 2009. She can also be found at www.simplyorganizedonline.com where she challenges herself to become more tech savvy with every project!